ITALY
UNDER GLASS

Marcie Layton

Copyright © 2021 Marcie Layton
First published 2021, Huge Jam
All rights reserved.
ISBN: 978-1-911249-69-6

This memoir has been written with the best intentions, to recount an exceptional time in my life. I believe I have recounted my story faithfully and truthfully. Names have been changed where appropriate. If memory has failed me at any point then I ask my readers' understanding and indulgence.

Designed and formatted by www.hugejam.com
Cover art *In the Deckchair Wire* by www.ceciliagatehouse.co.uk

*"These are the two faces of Italy:
the sacred and the social, the wine and the beer,
the art and the football, the style and the stolid,
the choirs and the klaxons…"*

Marcie Layton, Journal Entry, Italy 2018

Wiltshire Woes

The sound of tent pegs being hammered echoed across the valley. Our garden was crawling with men from the marquee hire company. As they unfolded the marquee sides, its clear plastic windows crackled, and the heavy panels of tent sides scraped across the lawn.

The weather forecast for Wiltshire was not good – I knew that – but I decided to ignore it, because I had a weekend of catering events planned – both professional and private – and a marquee would make all the difference. We had just moved here, so I didn't know what to expect from the weather in March; I just assumed that because it was quite far south, the weather would be milder than North Wales, where I had lived for many years.

Our house was very old, a converted farmhouse hunkered down low at the top of an impressive avenue of ancient trees. Behind us was a large, glorious Grade I listed manor house, and we were new tenants on the estate. The sweeping avenue of trees could be seen from the front of the manor. Our little cottage was tucked discreetly off to one side, not seen from the manor house, but sharing their lovely view. The idea was to pin this marquee discreetly to the front of the house, covering the front door, so guests could arrive in the lane behind us, and pass through the house directly into the marquee, taking in the views through the arched, Georgian style plastic windows.

I sat in the kitchen proofreading my menus for the weekend, trying to concentrate. It was too exciting, seeing a room being created out of thin air, and my mind kept wandering as I stared out the window, picturing the guests we had invited, and the meals I had planned, for this new sunny space

Friday morning was the Bradford-upon-Avon Business Breakfast, one of a series of networking breakfasts organised by businesses to support local tradespeople. I had volunteered to host a breakfast, which was also going to be the launch of my new business, *Moveable Feast Catering Company*.

I loved doing breakfasts. Not the traditional egg/bacon/sausage/fried bread type of breakfast, but what I refer to as "Extended Continental". MY breakfast would include: warm croissants stuffed with scrambled eggs & crispy pancetta; zucchini bread; cranberry walnut bread; Earl Grey bara brith; Moroccan spiced poached fruit; rhubarb compote with yoghurt; strawberry butter, marmalade butter; and the usual offerings of coffee, decaf coffee, tea, decaf tea, and Sicilian blood orange juice.

Friday night was my eldest boy Dylan's 22nd birthday; he would be travelling down from Liverpool by train that afternoon. I was throwing a birthday dinner for him that evening, the second event to be hosted in the marquee, but this time the guests would be made up of friends and family. I was preparing *vincisgrassi*, his favourite, and a glorious birthday cake was being prepared by an artisan baker in the town.

I would then be hosting a brunch on Saturday, for the largest of the three parties, celebrating our 30th wedding anniversary. I would prepare a deconstructed California cobb salad; poached salmon salad; new potato, egg, & bacon salad; and a pear, Roquefort, walnut, watercress & endive salad. We didn't know anyone in Wiltshire; all of our guests were travelling some distance to celebrate with us. Some would be staying with us in the house and a few more would be just down the lane in a local B&B.

A weather warning for snow was not at all what I'd pictured when

I planned the weekend, so I just focused on preparing the best food I could manage, doubling up on the coffee and tea. The same baker was designing a celebratory cake for this as well, a small top tier of fruit cake, a larger tier of chocolate sponge, half iced and half 'naked', dusted with icing sugar and trimmed with fresh berries. Two celebration cakes in one weekend was probably gilding the lily but I didn't care. Three parties in three days was heaven for me, and I thought we should really push the boat out, *sod the calories*.

The weekend would be rounded off with a farewell brunch on Sunday, before people went home. Late afternoon on Sunday a final pair of friends from London would be visiting for a high tea.

My taste in catering was influenced by my upbringing in California: lots of fresh vegetables and salads, fresh fruit, colourful, and informally displayed. Perhaps I was too optimistic about the arrival of spring when I planned these menus, as I was visualising a warm sunny morning for the breakfast, and a long, lingering vernal sunset for the anniversary.

Vincisgrassi was always going to be the choice for the birthday party; it's my son's all-time favourite. It is a particularly rich version of lasagne, from the Marche region of Italy. It is a voluptuous dish, thick with pork and beef mince, Parma ham, sautéed bacon, dried porcini and fresh mushrooms in cream. As the wind began to pick up and the thermometer dipped, I began to wish I'd made bucket loads of hot, comforting vincisgrassi for the entire weekend. It was perfect cold-weather stuff.

The marquee was completed at last. It looked exactly as I had imagined it would. Just several degrees colder than I had hoped. I began to dress the room for the first of the three events.

I had used a catering hire service for many items, and they had delivered three large round tables, stacks of chairs, and crates of crystal, china, cutlery, and linens. I roamed around our house looking for additional methods of warming it up. An ungainly portable gas heater was tucked into a corner, kettles were strategically placed right at the entrance, and large catering hot plates were laid out. The tall wooden coat stand suddenly looked minute, and I wondered if it would collapse under the weight of twenty-five winter coats.

I wanted my guests to be comfortable, but I had to trust that they would dress appropriately for the occasion. *This is Britain*, I reassured myself. *People know how to dress for winter*. I had stopped in Aldi and bulk-bought a big basket full of thick winter socks as party favours for the anniversary brunch on Saturday, just in case any guests wanted to walk their dogs down the avenue.

The business meeting was scheduled as a breakfast, there wasn't anything I could do about that, so I pushed to the back of my mind the observation that most sensible people prefer eating their breakfasts inside in cold weather. But my kitchen wasn't big enough for them all, not even my kitchen and lounge combined. We were all just going to have to grin and bear it.

Outside.

In the marquee.

In the cold.

I probably should just serve hot coffee and porridge.

The flowers arrived. They were stunning, a little bit of elegance mixed with country charm, in varying shades of neutrals and pastels, designed to co-ordinate with my floral top cloths. After I arranged the centrepieces for each of the tables, the flowers stood bolt upright in the cold air, as if in shock.

The cakes arrived, and I decided to store them in the tent, which by now seemed just as chill as my refrigerator. The seats of the chairs were glacial, as were the china plates and the silver flatwear; everything felt so unwelcoming. The fumes from the unsightly gas cylinder turned chill the minute they hit the frosty air.

Occasionally the wind would pick up, scraping the tent flaps and snapping the plastic windows back and forth. There were gaps between the panels and icy fingers of cold slid in and circled the inside of the tent. I took some final photos and scurried back into the warm kitchen to start early preparations for the breakfast, thawing myself out by the Rayburn.

It all looked great. It all felt terrible. It was *Baltic*.

The morning of the breakfast I awoke eye-wateringly early, feeling a curious mixture of excitement and dread. There was no sign of snow but the ice was evident everywhere; I wasn't sure how easy it would be for cars to climb the steep hill out of Bradford-upon-Avon. I had asked Glyn, my teenaged younger son, to stand outside near the layby, directing traffic and guiding cars to parking places. I tried not to think about how frozen he was going to be. I had a stack of laminated car parking signs; I needed to find somewhere to display them which wasn't covered with ice.

I double-checked the marquee for the sixth time in an hour. It all looked so beautiful, and so frosty. The three large round tables were now each laid out with flower arrangements, my floral top cloths, the white catering cloths peeping out from underneath, shining silver flatware and the wink of crystal glasses. The freezing temperatures brought out the colours in high relief: pale pastels so redolent of the English countryside.

The hiss of the gas spewed unappetising fumes into the tent and across the dining tables. It made absolutely no difference whatsoever. A small domestic oil-fired heater sat glaring at it from the other side of the room.

I had placed the hot drinks station just inside the entrance to the marquee, and I smacked the plastic milk bottles hard on the tent floor to dislodge the ice brick forming inside. The white china cups looked crisp, professional, but were painfully chill to the touch. I used a mittened hand to wipe frost from the windows and was thrilled to see that a staggeringly beautiful sunrise had appeared out of nowhere, pastel dawn hues complementing my colour scheme.

The marquee was damp and running with condensation. I tried to pull the gaps in the tent panels as close together as I could but they were only designed to provide cursory protection from the elements, not a barrier to snowdrifts.

A very sleepy Glyn, finally emerged, bleary-eyed, and I bribed him with hot chocolate and the promise of warm pastries. It was finally time to start displaying the morning's menu, and I criss-crossed back and forth in front of the noxious heater, bringing out tray after tray of breakfast foods into the igloo.

Just time for one last panicked vision of all twenty-five guests huddled around the green Rayburn holding steaming cups of perfect coffee... *Why hadn't we rented a house with a bigger kitchen? Should I restrict entrance to five people at a time: ushering them in one door, seating them briefly in the warm kitchen, shoving a plate of food in their hands, and herding them back out into the freezing morning air and waving in the next lot, like a conveyor belt...*

Then I heard a car approach. It was showtime, folks.

I don't think I've ever met a friendlier group of strangers in my life. That lovely British stiff-upper-lip, World War-winning quality, filled my ice brick tent with jovial *bonhomie*. People arrived, smiling, giggling as they unwrapped themselves from layers of scarves, hats, and mittens. I needn't have worried about the coat stand – it was empty – because everybody kept their coats on.

Everybody had funny marquee stories to tell: sodden wedding receptions, sweltering anniversary celebrations, frozen birthdays. It was a universal talking point and brought us all together, our little band of local businesspeople supporting each other, empathising with me about the challenges of the catering industry.

I peered out once into the makeshift car park, saw iced windscreens and my frozen child, decided to focus on what I could control, and scampered back into the kitchen for another pot of coffee.

It was only a breakfast, and before I knew it, it was over. There weren't any no-shows; I'd had a full house. People loved the food, laughed about the cold, and I was left with a warm and cosy feeling that my new career was going to be a success.

We waved off the last of the guests. I then staggered sleepily to the kitchen sink and turned my attention to the washing up. I had a birthday party to prepare for in less than ten hours.

The sunlight was dazzling, pouring through the large windows. It added no warmth at all, but it was cheering and glorious. I turned off the hired gas cylinder to save fuel for the next two events, and the silence was so peaceful. I bundled up all of the linens and stuffed them into the clothes washer, roughly three loads in total. The washing up was pretty large too: twenty-five glasses, twenty-five coffee cups and saucers, twenty-five dinner plates and side plates and bowls and cutlery and serving platters, all needed to be run through the dishwasher, or hand washed, and wiped and prepared for the party on Saturday.

We were only eight friends and family for the birthday, so it was more relaxed. I had made the vincisgrassi in advance for heating, the cake was cold but brilliant, and I felt more human after I'd had a nap.

Whatever temperature issues we were having by day were exacerbated by sundown. In hindsight, if my ego hadn't been running rampant I would've laid out the meal in the kitchen. It wasn't huge, but we could've all fit snugly, had a quick supper inside, watching the exterior of the tent whipping loudly in the wind from the kitchen window. Maybe we could've had cake in front of the roaring fire.

But I had rented this marquee and I was damn well going to get my money's worth out of it.

So on went the gas heater (hiss hiss), out came the family silver candelabra, and I laid a table again with the frozen cutlery. I hadn't accounted for lighting, really. Sort of forgot about it. It was dim in there, dim and damp and chilly. It looked quite pretty with the candles lit, and they didn't blow out as frequently as I'd expected, considering the draft whistling through the gaps in the tent flaps. It wasn't exactly the right style of event for a young man's birthday, but he was very understanding about it.

I believe firmly in choosing flexible meals when I have guests who are travelling some distance to visit us. There's nothing worse than having people arrive, having been stuck in traffic for hours, to find a meal waiting for them overcooked, dried out, black on top.

Vincisgrassi is ideal on a travel day; just needs a quick bung in the oven to reheat gently. Most of our family had arrived, made a quick inspection of the igloo, and snuggled down by the fire. But one couple, Phillipa and Leonard, were late. I wasn't too worried because Phillipa had lived nearby as a child, and knew the area.

Or so I thought.

Normally I wouldn't put anything in to reheat until everyone had arrived, but it was getting late and we had a big day planned on Saturday so, against my better judgement, I start reheating the vincisgrassi. We waited. The weather worsened. I blew out the candles, and began to worry about the amount of gas being pumped into an empty marquee. I threw more coal on the fire inside the house. The clock ticked. We waited some more. Left phone messages. My temper began to swell.

Finally, we heard the crack of a door knocker and they were in the kitchen, poor Phillipa and Leonard, frazzled, dripping, pale. Leonard held a damp overnight bag and a bottle of champagne, protruding out of the bottom of a torn, saturated paper bottle bag.

Phillipa looked crestfallen.

"I'm so, so sorry everybody. I know this area like the back of my hand. Well, I did. When I was six." She wiped away a damp strand of hair. "I just wanted to pop by and see my old house. I think the area's changed a bit over the years. I remember we used to turn left at an old stone barn…"

Her voice trailed off as she caught my expression.

"Well, we're here now anyway. Happy birthday, Dylan." She smiled weakly and gave him a hug, sliding a box of chocolates into his hand. Leonard shook his umbrella, sending spray hissing onto the Rayburn.

"Let's eat" I said, tersely. I tried to put on my Happy Face but I couldn't quite pull it off. I felt so ungracious. I hated it when I got like that.

I was getting tired, and worried, and angry. I was being unreasonable, I knew that, and that insight made me even angrier. I was mad about the weather, mad about my late guests, mad about the marquee, mad about life. I mean, everybody gets lost, *I get lost*, my friends were not unique in this, but why did they have to get lost on the way to *my special party*, during *my special weekend*?

I tried to put on a welcoming veneer of hospitality, but everybody could sense that I was really pissed off; I could only manage a frosty demeanour. I was ashamed of my own reaction but the feelings were too big to handle and my resistance was low.

Everyone reluctantly filed into the marquee, grabbing their coats and hats from the radiators as they passed.

"Glyn, please could you light the candles?" I handed him a small box of matches and disappeared into the kitchen, dreading the moment when I would open the oven door.

The glass dish was charred; the meat looked like liquorice. I stared at our meal, utterly carcinogenic. Thoughts of *Burger King* flitted through my mind.

"Sod it," I muttered, and grabbed the dish.

"Happy birthday, sweetheart" I said apologetically, sweeping into the marquee in my parka, brandishing the casserole dish, wearing ski gloves. My entrance snuffed out two of the candles on the candelabra.

"Glyn, please could you relight those candles?"

I smiled with artificial brightness.

"Peter, could I ask you please to pour the wine? Use a torch if it's too dark to see."

Peter took the corkscrew in one hand and tucked the torch under his other arm; it promptly winked and went out.

"Batteries please, Dylan; in the Daddy drawer in the kitchen. Two big batteries"

Dylan made a hasty exit, glancing worriedly into the casserole dish.

"What's that?" Glyn said, peering through the gloom at the vincisgrassi.

"Don't you remember? It's Dylan's favourite!"

Glyn sat back, irritated. "It looks black. Just a small piece for me. I'll have extra cake."

We all sat down to a dried out and unappetising meal. With no electric lighting overhead, we could barely make out each other's faces. Conversation sputtered and stalled. Two pairs of three-stemmed candelabra struggled valiantly against the gloom, but six little candles were no match for the cold shadows that plagued us. I hacked away at the pasta base with a variety of kitchen utensils, chipping it away from the sides of the dish.

Eating a cake in virtual darkness is tricky, as you never really know where the icing is, and it's a challenge to keep the cake on the fork, but once in the mouth it was truly divine, and at least the baker kept his reputation as an *artisan* baker intact.

Just before I went to sleep I glanced at my notes in preparation for all three events: pages of *Pinterest* boards with recipe ideas, hospitality ideas, event planning tips. I had had such high hopes and wanted to be bustling about with lots of energy. But the cold began to wear me down and sap my strength. I was known for hosting events that were fun and even a little crazy, but there was something a bit sour and mean about this one, as I constantly battled the elements and lost my sense of joy about it all.

That's when the snow hit.

I'd been peering out occasionally during the evening looking for flurries, but Mother Nature kindly let me get to sleep before spilling her load onto us. Our bedraggled late arrivals were staying in the master bedroom, and we'd juggled rooms around with our boys; our other guests were staying locally. I felt ashamed, in retrospect, about laying on a not-too-brilliant-in-the-end-birthday event for poor Dylan. In the planning stages it had looked like it was going to be a brilliant weekend of fun and festivities but somehow events, and the weather, overwhelmed me.

I couldn't quite see what the outside was like, as our bedroom was down a long corridor with a tiny window, but as I picked my way downstairs, the full horror of it all revealed itself through the kitchen window.

Large drifts of white snow weighed down the top of the marquee and iced the tops of the dry-stone walls. The car was covered, the land was obscured, the ancient avenue of trees top heavy with white icing. But even the kitchen window scene couldn't have prepared me for the sight greeting me when I opened our front door into the marquee.

Snow had blown into the tent through the large canvas flaps. *There was a small snowdrift up against the gas cylinder.* The coat stand had a light dusting. My grandmother's silver tea set was frosted with snow, and the hot water urn and tea kettle had tiny drifts of their own. The packets of tea and coffee neatly laid out were obscured. The milk was frozen solid. The half-iced and half-naked celebration cake looked brittle and hard as a rock.

I stifled a sob; nobody else was awake yet. I was alone here in my little battle against the elements.

Once, many years ago, when my husband and I were unpacking Christmas decorations, a little water filled snow globe had fallen and broken open. We stood there, staring at it, not knowing what to do first: dry up the water, pick up the broken bits of glass, sweep up the fake snow, rescue the decorations inside.

I thought of this while staring at my party venue, reminiscent of an episode of *Pingu*.

The poor little oil-filled heater had been chugging away pointlessly all night, but I warmed my hands against it as I tried to figure out what to do first. The rest of the guests were coming at lunchtime, only a few hours away.

I channelled British stoicism, and suddenly sprang into life. I photographed everything in its white and snowy state, knowing that one day I would laugh about it all. I hoped and prayed that the gas cylinder would last, as I set about clearing the snow from the interior of the tent.

Perhaps now is a good time to tell you why I was here, in Wiltshire, shovelling snow out of a hired marquee.

We used to live in Anglesey, in a pretty little restored cottage on the coast. My hopes and dreams had been pinned on opening a healthy-option take-away café, offering fresh salads, soups, and smoothies to beach day-trippers, water-sports enthusiasts, and ramblers on the Anglesey Coastal Path. It was an inspired idea – offering healthy food to active people – but my neighbours didn't agree. They had all moved to the neighbourhood to escape the stresses and strains of modern life, and once they had staked their claim to part of that magical, beachy neighbourhood, they wanted to make sure that nothing disturbed their tranquillity.

The local council rejected my application to open the cafe, citing the fact that I was in a residential neighbourhood. My neighbours had actually written to the council and objected as well. The fact that at least half of the buildings near me were holiday lettings – running as businesses in a residential neighbourhood – seemed to have escaped everybody's notice.

I decided not to appeal. If I had won second time around I would still have to live with these people, and I suspected that they could easily make my life, and my business, a misery. It seemed the best option was to pick up sticks and go somewhere else, leaving my little seaside dreams behind.

I put my house on the market and trawled through business listings throughout the whole of the U.K., trying to find a leasehold business which was already established, so that I could slip in as new management and not have to face dissent from any of my neighbours. One day I came across a listing in Bradford-upon-Avon, Wiltshire, and my heart stopped.

There was a listing for a little restaurant, available for lease. It was achingly pretty – handsome, actually – placed right on the river by the ancient bridge. Large picture windows afforded river views of ducks and reeds and lichen-bedecked ancient stone. It was the perfect size, the perfect price, the perfect dream.

All I needed to do was sell my beach house and I'd be happy as Larry.

We found a lovely house to rent nearby, and relocated down south to the stunning Wiltshire countryside, but still the beach house didn't sell. I was having increasingly fraught conversations with the agent handling the lease, but I was really helpless. I shouldn't have applied to lease a business until the house I was using to finance the project was sold.

By now my pretty little fisherman's cottage was becoming a millstone round my neck.

One day the phone rang. It was the agent for the restaurant

building. Somebody else had got the restaurant, someone with cash in hand and the freedom to move quickly. I was gutted. I was trying to overcome the anger and frustration at my failed business plans, and all the joy I had experienced in my coastal cottage had disappeared.

We loved the area we had moved to, a town known for artisan food specialists, a thriving tourist industry, and a love of good food.

Once in Wiltshire, looking at the local leasehold prices and the general lay of the land, I decided that catering from home was the wiser move, and so with our landlord's blessing, I created *Moveable Feast Catering Company*.

Which is what led me to my marquee, in the snow, and a luncheon event looming ominously in a few hours' time.

The wedding anniversary lunch was going to be more relaxed, I decided, made up as it was of friends and family and not like the professional event launching my new catering business. My immediate family had already been broken in by the icy supper the night before so they knew what to expect when they woke up. The others would learn soon enough when they arrived.

I began to get phone calls and messages from my guests. Were the roads passable? Was there any parking? Was it still snowing? Had the grit trucks been by? Fuelled by endless cups of tea I did my best to exude a sort of benign and philosophical attitude. People could make the journey if they wanted to, but we completely understood if they stayed at home.

I no longer offered any resistance to events as they unfolded. A snow plough could have driven straight through the centre of the tent at this point, flattening the celebration cake on its way, and I wouldn't have minded. An avalanche could have enveloped the entire house and I would have simply watched, smiling weakly, coffee in hand, wrapped in my Parka. I had now transcended a philosophical attitude and was just existing, going with the flow, riding the crest of the wave smiling and waving.

As it happened, it was actually a lovely afternoon. The good old team spirit that had infused my business breakfast guests was instilled in my family and friends as well.

We were finally defeated by the marquee. People would arrive, dusted in snow, commiserate about the weather, stroll into the marquee and then make a hasty retreat. The smell of gas and the chill in the air was just too much.

People preferred to pack in like sardines in front of the blazing fire in the lounge, rather than stretch out comfortably in the glacial marquee. There were guests on the sofa, guests on the floor, guests in the kitchen warming themselves by the Rayburn, sitting next to piles of washing up in the kitchen sink, guests wandering about the house with no fixed abode, *but at least they were warm*.

By sundown my nerves were shot. We had dropped our boys off at the train station and they went off, respectively to Liverpool for work and to Cardiff for university. On the departure of a final pair of friends who had joined us for tea and cake late afternoon – all of us laughing and joking about the Ice Follies I had just hosted – I collapsed onto the sofa by the fire and had a little think.

The house was so quiet now. No friends. No family. No children. Just Peter, and me, and the dog. And a ton of leftover celebration cake.

Why was I doing this? Why was I making salad-based menus, in Britain, in the snow? Why was I planning al fresco events and then shrouding them in plastic and canvas due to inclement weather? I felt like I was pretending to have a sort of lifestyle which I didn't actually have: a Mediterranean lifestyle.

I think sometimes when you get very, very tired, something just snaps inside and you begin to think more clearly. Or maybe you're just too tired to hang onto your old preconceptions about what your life should be like.

I loved the village we were living in, and I loved nearby Bradford-upon-Avon, and I loved living in the English countryside, but was it really me? My salads were frozen to their salad bowls. My floral arrangements had frostbite. I suddenly felt that I needed to be somewhere warm. Somewhere sunny. Somewhere else.

And then I remembered Italy.

My go-to destination, always, for holidays. We all loved Italy; we'd been there several times. Who could possibly forget the sun, scenery, fabulous food, a warm and welcoming population?

I suddenly had a little vision of a life in Italy. A little Italianate lightning bolt if you will. Flash! Boom! Italy!!

We should move to Italy.

Our children were nearly grown, caught up in their various early twenty-something lives. They no longer lived with us. It felt at the time that they no longer needed us. Our eldest boy was living with his girlfriend and working in a school in Liverpool. Our youngest was in a dorm full of friends in Cardiff University, having a fantastic time. I was left holding the tent peg in the snow, in Wiltshire.

We should reinvent ourselves in Italy. Why not?

I glanced over at Peter, sitting in the big armchair, reading the news online. He looked pretty wrecked as well. He was twenty years my senior, and probably wasn't too keen on recreating the sort of weekend that had just passed.

"Peeee-terrr?" I said in a cajoling, and slightly whiny voice.

"Ye-e-es?" He replied, suspiciously.

"I have a crazy little idea."

"Oh dear. This sounds expensive."

I warmed to my theme, excitement building, as I prepared myself to launch the Italian Campaign.

"Can I just – look – wait, just hear me out. I have this crazy little idea but it wouldn't really cost us too much, I don't think, and it might actually make us some money."

He had been on the verge of nodding off, eyelids beginning to droop. It was a good time to slip a suggestion across, when he was too sleepy to resist.

"Do you want to move to Italy?"

The Plan

Peter's eyes opened wide. He glanced sidelong at me.
"Italy?"
"Yeah," I said, eagerly. "Italy."

He sat forward in the armchair, fully awake now. "Tell me more," he said carefully.

"Well," I said, warming to my theme. "If the beach house doesn't sell soon, why don't we use the bridging loan we'd gotten for the restaurant, to buy a house in Italy instead? It would be a fantastic plus for my catering business, to have links with a country like Italy. I could learn more about Italian cookery to expand my menus over here."

I was on a roll.

"I could write cookery blogs. I could even run a cookery school!" I was barely seated now, it was so exciting. "*Moveable Feast Catering Company*: it's already perfect!"

We looked at each other, smiling.

"We could spend half a year abroad and half a year here," he countered, perhaps not wanting to leave England completely.

"The boys would love it! Italian holidays! Italian food! Italian weather!" A half-charred log shifted loudly in the fireplace, sending off sparks.

"We've got a good idea how much we can expect from the beach house, so we'll set a budget and stick to it. I bet the property values are pretty good over there, at least in the country, maybe not the cities."

Peter sat back in the armchair, and I could tell he had visions of *carbonara, insalata tricolore,* and *Montepulciano* running through his head. I grabbed my phone and googled on *Rightmove Overseas*, plugged a price limit into the search engine. Almost instantly the most glorious houses began to appear: small tumble-down villas, going for a song, frescoed apartments with terraces and lovely views, dubious mounds of earth with only a wall left standing.

"Oh!" I cried, "Ooh, look at this one! Oh my God look at that! *Peter, just look at these!!"*

He gestured across for the phone, and I handed it over, realising I now didn't have a device to look at the *Rightmove* listings. I raced into the kitchen for my tablet – past the snow laden marquee – ignoring the mountains of dirty dishes and soiled table linens, due to be returned to the catering hire company early the next morning. All the exhaustion of the weekend had melted away, in the first flush of *The Italian Campaign.*

I flew into the lounge and plonked myself back onto the sofa.

"Which part of Italy?" Peter wondered, scrolling down the listings.

"I dunno, I think Tuscany's probably out; too expensive. Everybody from England seems to go to Tuscany. We love the Amalfi Coast! Do you think we could afford a beach house near Positano?"

Peter scrolled further down the listings, humming under his breath.

"No."

"Oh, why not?"

"No. Way out of our price range. Nothing even remotely near the beach."

"Here's a lovely fixer-upper, near, uh, L' Aquila, where's that?"

"That was the location of that terrible earthquake a few years back that buried the whole village," was his deadpan answer.

"Oh. Okay. So not L'Aquila."

I googled "earthquake zones in Italy". There were actually some parts of Italy that were not prone to earthquakes, and rather a lot that looked incredibly unstable. But I did recognise a few names from the property listings I'd just been trawling through, and I realised that that was why they were tumble-down, and going for a song.

"Right, let's set some parameters here, we've got to plug in more than the upper price limit; *there's tons of properties here.*"

Suddenly, I couldn't help myself. I dropped my phone in my lap and opened my arms wide.

"*VOLARE!*" I bellowed, singing in a rusty, out-of-practice belt voice, "*Oh-oh! Cantare, Wo wo wo wo!!*"

The dog twitched. Thank goodness she was deaf. And thank goodness we had no close neighbours.

I couldn't think straight. Exhaustion plus excitement equals chaos. We'd been to several of the traditional Italian holiday places, and still an enormous part of the country was unexplored. We'd visited Grave-in-Chianti, Tuscany, Amalfi, Positano, Pisa, the Veneto, Sienna, Lucca, Florence, and Venice. Never even touched the boot of the country. I'd never seen the Lakes. Or Sicily.

I'd always harboured a wish to travel on a culinary tour through Italy. We had home-educated our boys when they were small, and at one point we had studied – and grazed our way through – recipes from every single region. We learned about the rich butter and cream-laden recipes of the far North, and working our way down to the hot, dry, arid southern regions, preparing recipes smothered in olive oil, garlic and basil. I had only read about the great metamorphosis from North to South. I wanted to live it for myself.

I finally had to restrain myself, get a grip, and clear away the carnage of the last three days' events. I was too tired to sleep, too tired to stay awake. I really wanted to thumb through every single Italian cookbook I had looking for inspiration. Finally the last load of dishes went into the dishwasher, the last champagne flute was wiped dry, the linens were bundled into an enormous ball, and most of the ice-topped furniture had been carted out of the marquee. We had been given a little fig tree as an anniversary gift. It had the tiniest little wink of a fig on it. I took this to be a good omen, a sign that Italy was somehow really on the cards for us.

The next morning, I prepared a huge cup of coffee, sat down by the fire, and began to trawl through the listings. Just for fun I went to the Rightmove search engine but didn't put in an upper price limit. The properties available were mesmerizing. Suddenly, coastal properties sprang up which hadn't appeared when I'd put our budget in. The most dazzling estates were available, palazzos in Rome, villas in Perugia, dreamy Venetian apartments on the Grand Canal, Sicilian townhouses. I mouthed the words silently to myself: Lombardy, Abruzzo, Campania, Lazio, Friuli- Venezia Giulia. Soon I would be able to put a face to a name, stand in these glorious regions and perhaps call one of them home.

We put together a wish list of some criteria to narrow down the search. Suddenly I felt like an expert on the country, and made some pretty outlandish assumptions about what might suit us best.

"It shouldn't be too remote," I decided, waggling a pencil at Peter. "You won't be very comfortable driving on the wrong side of the road, so we should probably only look at places in towns or cities where we can walk to the local shops."

Any degree of introspection would have alerted me to the fact that it was I who wouldn't be happy driving on the wrong side of the road. It didn't really cross my mind that, once you we there, and with a left-hand drive Italian car, you would be on the right side of the road, just like everybody, and driving would be easy-peasy-lemon-squeezy.

We wanted minimum two bedrooms, open fireplace, not too many stairs, and some sort of garden or terrace for al fresco dining. Just like everybody else who was looking in Italy, no doubt. Initially I was hoping to do without a car (still afraid of the wrong side of the road), so a town location was preferred. Big cities were out. No noise, no air pollution, no traffic jams. It had to be old, old, old.

I kept putting fixer-uppers on the short-list because they looked like such good value, but my wiser husband took most of them off again. "I'm getting a bit too old for a fixer-upper", he warned. "We've been there, done that in Wales. Yes it was fun, but it was also tiring and expensive. And I'm not too keen on hiring local builders long distance from over here, to do extensive renovations for us."

The Big Trawl for properties took a day or two, and finally yielded a small selection within our budget. There were four in Lazio – south of Rome – and two in Perugia. We looked at each other one morning after breakfast, as I prepared to contact our first estate agent. There was so much to consider: cars, flights, water, Euros, *the language*, everything. All the listings were in Euros, and I sort of lost track of the conversion from British Pound Sterling. I absolutely had to keep within our budget, but it was so easy to stray slightly upwards, thinking to myself that *I could always talk them down*.

The snow had melted. The marquee had gone back. The champagne flutes were stored safely back in their little cupboard. The little fig tree grew slowly each day. I emailed two estate agents and waited impatiently for a reply, checking my phone a dozen times an hour for a message.

My living status was slightly unusual. Peter was British, the boys were British, but I was an ex-pat American and held an American passport. I'd lived and worked in Britain for nearly thirty years, and I hoped that despite my U.S. passport, I might be treated as a European when it came to purchasing a property abroad.

I finally got a reply from two estate agents: Giada in Perugia and Viv in Lazio. Giada was very Italian, Viv was Australian. Giada's English was excellent, and she worked for a very elegant, sophisticated, and very large property group. Viv, I deduced, was a small two-man band working alongside her husband Mario.

All of the candidates for viewings were fabulous, to my mind, but the Queen of the Viewings was the *Palazzo* in Arpino. I didn't understand how it could possibly be within our meagre little €110,000 budget. It had frescoes. High ceilings. A grand staircase. I figured that it must really need a lot of work. Peter took it off the list. I put it back on. Off it went. On it went. It was like a comedy routine.

When I sent my wish list to Viv she wrote back immediately. There must be some mistake. The Palazzo was not in our budget. I wrote back, insisting that it was. She wrote back, citing a list price of €1,100,000. I stared at the email. There must have been a typo in the property listing. It wasn't a steal at €110,000. It was never a steal at all. It was exactly what it should have been, at over a million.

I had a tiny, niggling worry in the back of my mind that we'd been tricked somehow, lured into contacting them with the promise of a fixer-upper of a Palazzo which in fact was ten times over our budget. Maybe this was an estate agent ruse. That was a bit paranoid, I told myself.

The next night I woke up in a cold sweat, in the middle of the night. I'd been dreaming about earthquakes. I had lived through one or two when I was a kid in California, and it wasn't an experience I'd relish having again. I had an early morning blast on my computer, reading up on Italian earthquakes. They were serious. They were very real. They were a constant threat. Some of the geological maps I looked up showed glaring red markings where the major fault lines were, many of them criss-crossing areas where we had been looking for property. The area we were looking in was just outside a big red area. I was shaken, but not stirred.

I wrote to Viv about my concerns, and she wrote back confirming that yes, in some areas it was not safe, but in the areas where we were looking we should be fine. She pointed out that for any property, the construction of the building, the materials with which it was built, and the age of the building were key factors. She mentioned earthquake chains. The Italians were in the habit of wrapping vulnerable buildings in enormous, thick chains, right round the perimeter of the building, to keep them secure in an earthquake.

I tried to picture it: a building wrapped in a chain. I hadn't seen any chains in the property listings. I thought she was slightly bonkers. You couldn't possibly just whip a chain around a building. I decided she was having me on.

While all of this correspondence was going on, I was still developing my catering business in Wiltshire. I had one regular catering job, a result of my frosty breakfast launch. I was writing blogs about local food related companies, advertising, creating menus and cookery course brochures. Spring had finally arrived in earnest, and the snow was long gone. I really began to appreciate the stunning beauty of Wiltshire, once I realised that soon I would be leaving it.

Bath was a fascination for me. The mellow Bath stone was so enticing. It made every sort of building just that little bit more elegant. I was amused to realise that what I was looking at – Classical architecture – was not English architecture at all, but a pinch from the Italians. It's so easy to look at a classical Georgian column, or a balustrade, and think "Oh, that's so very English." But the love affair between England and Italy is very old, and it seems that the ancient Romans were just as entranced by English Bath – because of its healing waters – as the English were entranced by Rome. Palladio had a major impact in both countries.

My contact with Giada was just as exciting. She was very friendly and helpful. She was based in Spoleto, home to an incredible annual music festival, which I thought would be a real plus should we choose one of her properties to buy. One of her listings made my heart melt. It was a little townhouse created from a series of converted farm buildings in Piegaro, near Perugia. It had contemporary hand-painted frescoes on the walls, and was in a little commune, with a shared pool. A second house, nearer Spoleto, had a stunning terrace.

We finally narrowed down our shortlist to four properties on Viv's books, and two on Giada's. I sat at the kitchen table, so proud, scrolling over and over again through the lovely homes, trying to picture us in each of the houses.

And then I saw the house in Colli. It was perfect. 17th century. Three bedrooms. Vaulted ceilings. Enormous stone staircase. Views to die for. It was the end wing of an ancient palazzo belonging to a noble family in a small rural village an hour and a half south of Rome. A little bit of country but walking distance to the local shop. I squinted my eyes and I could just picture myself *there*, in the sitting room, *there* making supper in that kitchen, *there* on the terrace with Campari, watching the sun go down.

There were two properties listed next to each other, the palazzo townhouse, and below it, an unconverted coach house. It was possible to buy the two together, which was a wonderful idea as they were on top of each other, but our budget only extended to one, so we hoped that the coach house didn't go to someone unpleasant who would be living right underneath us.

The five Lazio properties were all more or less near a town with the romantic name: Monte San Giovanni Campano. It was impossible to say that name without giving it a little Italianate lilt: *MONte San GioVANNi CamPANo!* I roamed around the house, danced with the dog saying *MONte San GioVANNi CamPANo!* At breakfast Peter and I would say it to each other: *MONte San GioVANNi CamPANo!* I mouthed to myself our new address: "Peter and Marcie Layton, *MONte San GioVANNi CamPANo, LAZio, ITALia.*" It was thrilling.

Peter booked the flights. Found a nice little hotel – central to all of the Lazio properties – and an equivalent hotel in Spoleto for our visit to Giada. We were going to fly into Rome, take the train out to the Lazio hotel, have Viv drive us around to the viewings, then take the train to Spoleto where Giada would show us the other two. Apparently, no matter where you wanted to travel in and around Rome, you needed to travel into Central Rome in order to get there. But it was all doable by train and saved hiring a car.

There was no post-entertainment slump for me. I never came down off the three-party-weekend at all. *We were going to Italy.* That thought took all of my energy, all of my concentration, all of my passion.

I grabbed all my Italian cookery books and researched Lazio. The Lazio houses which we were due to look at were all in a region called Ciociaria, named after a traditional shepherd's shoe. I plugged it into three separate pronunciation websites and all three of them had little recordings that pronounced the word differently. I decided to avoid using the word if at all possible.

It was beautiful, rugged countryside, with steep sharp distinctive-looking conical mountains. The regional ingredients were simple but delicious: rich olive oil, ewe's milk Pecorino, Prosciutto, lamb, Mortadella sausage, tomatoes, peppers, a unique little anise-flavoured sweet biscuit. It wasn't a beef region, or a wine-making region. Lazio had a coastline but not near where we were looking. In fact, the town of MONte San GioVANNi CamPANo was known as "The Town of Olives". Nearby Arpino was know as the "City of

Culture" because Cicero was born there, and it had a tradition of supporting the arts.

It was magical.

Perugia looked divine as well. It has its own annual chocolate festival which in itself is a good reason to move there. The *Perugian EuroChocolate Festival*, and the *Spoleto Music Festival del Due Mondi*: what more could a girl want?

The days crawled by so slowly towards our visit. I made enormous Italian Project boards on *Pinterest*, and wandered around the house muttering snatches of my limited Italian vocabulary.

It is in my nature to fuss about the little things in life, and somehow miss the Big Picture. I started looking at paint colours and making lists of which furniture we wanted to take. We already discussed the fact that we would need a left-hand drive, and we would need to make at least one journey by car to bring the dog across. She was an ancient Wheaten terrier named Sandy – blind, deaf, on a soft food diet – but she was my very special dog and she was coming too. *Il mio adorabile cane.*

Viewings

After what seemed like an eternity, we were off to Rome. I felt very *special* as we queued in Bristol airport. Other people were going on that flight for their holidays. We were going there to live. *La Dolce Vita*. That was us.

I'm a very enthusiastic traveller in my head, but not necessarily in real life. I dream about the fun things – food, wine, beautiful hotel rooms – but get thrown by flight delays and queuing and lost luggage. Also, Peter struggles with disabilities and wasn't able to walk any great distance, which does make airports a daunting task.

The Bristol end of the flight was, well, a typical British airport experience, but once in Rome, the true charm of Italy began to reveal itself. Everybody was so considerate. So easy-going. So happy to help.

We had a booked a wheelchair for the long trek from the plane to the Roma Termini train towards Lazio. Once they realised that Peter had mobility problems we were treated like royalty. A quietly cheerful young airport attendant, with shoulder length flowing hair, briskly slid us through the terminal, humming under his breath. With a quick flip of his wrist he snapped open barrier gates that were only used for staff, and whisked us towards our train, using all manner of short cuts. He gossiped and chuckled with the Passport Control staff; you'd think he was sitting in a sports bar drinking a beer and not working in an airport.

The *Leonardo Express* is a train that links the airport to Rome Termini, a very quick and comfortable ride, and having changed trains, at last we were gliding through the Italian countryside towards Frosinone, our destination railway stop.

I went into some sort of cultural overload at this point. The contrast between our Wiltshire cottage and the mountains of Lazio was staggering. The train journey was long, an hour and a half, but it gave me time to adjust to our surroundings and take in the general ambience. I looked around at the train carriage filled with Italians, all quietly chatting, or reading, or snoozing. They didn't realise just how very special they were, how special this train carriage was, how special the little packets of olives with their cute little toothpicks were, which we had bought on the plane (Italian trains don't have food service). I was already turning into some sort of Italian *luvvy*. The scenery sped by quickly, but not so quickly that I couldn't make out ancient buildings, olive groves, snow-capped mountains in the distance.

I felt like I was in a movie.

Frosinone train station was unremarkable. We managed to find a taxi easily enough, although he wasn't too sure of our destination, which allowed me to then say, with great gusto, "MONte San GioVANNI CamPANo, por favore!"

Such fun, that.

The hotel which Peter had booked was in a tiny hamlet just outside Monte San Giovanni Campano, called *Colli*, which means *hills* in Italian. Frosinone had been a chaotic rush hour jumble, but as the taxi climbed out of the town on the *autostrada* the true nature of the Lazio countryside became apparent.

It was dry and arid, yet still quite green. The hills in the near distance were incredibly steep, sharp-peaked. In the far distance, the mountain range was very forbidding and ragged. There were a surprising number of half-built buildings, their metal internal girders poking out at odd angles. Between the half-built new-builds and the half-collapsed old buildings were a range of very beautiful farmhouses and country villas. I had read that many people who lived and worked in Roma during the year had summer places in Lazio – sometimes used only a few weeks out of the year – but to beat the intense Roman heat and air pollution, it was an understandable luxury.

We drove past the turning off to Monte San Giovanni Campano, and on down to little Colli beneath it. We noticed that the locals called it MSGC which seemed an appropriate shorthand. Soon we were in Colli, a charming little town built up astride the ridge of a long narrow hill. Houses on the left had staggering views across the Liri river valley. Houses on the right had staggering views off towards the mountains. Everybody had something.

Arriving at the driveway to the hotel, the *Ville del Colle*, we noticed that it was built across the top of its own little hill. The drive curled up around the hill in a spiral, and when we arrived at the top we realised that the hotel had 360 degree views, taking in the views of the river valley, and the mountains, and everything else in between.

I was very tired, very excited, and very happy to be at the hotel. We were greeted courteously by Andreas, the proprietor, a tall, soft-spoken man with a gracious demeanour. The hotel itself was of comparatively modern construction, post-war certainly. It had very large reception rooms and dining rooms, with a very large terrace for *al fresco* dining. The facilities included a lovely outdoor pool with incredible views, and poolside party venues.

We were given a choice of rooms and we chose one with another staggering view of the Liri river valley. Once the sun had set, the villages began to light up, encircling the tips of the hills with bright tiaras of light. Many of the ancient villages in this area were built high up on these steep hills for protection. We would discover that many would have treacherous windy roads leading to the top, and then stout village walls protecting the inhabitants within.

Our room was sparsely furnished and very clean. There was cool marble everywhere. The stone floors, chilly to the touch in April, would be soothing in the heat of summer. The hotel itself was strangely quiet. There was the distant sound of rock music further down the valley, a child's laughter drifting up through the window, birdsong, an occasional sheep or goat bleating.

I felt a strange disorientating feeling: not quite jet lag, but the sort of confusion you feel when you travel from one culture to another. I was too tired to worry about my lack of Italian. My culinary Italian was passable, but my everyday Italian was non-existent. Andreas rescued us with his good understanding of English.

As we came down for dinner, we were convinced that we were the only guests. The child's laughter was closer, and we could hear the murmur of happy voices. When we arrived in the entry hall, adjacent to the first restaurant, we saw that the only people in the room, seated at a large round table, were the whole of Andreas' family. Three generations of the Ville del Colle family were having dinner together, including little Georgio, Andreas's small son. He was being impish and delightful. His entire family gazed smiling at his every antic. I thought what a wonderful way to grow up: in a large hotel, with a swimming pool, surrounded by a family that adored him.

We were taken up a flight of stairs and seated outside on the terrace, gazing in awe at the pink ombré sunset spreading out before us. Everywhere around us was rosy gold, and warm.

Andreas came out to take our orders, but without menus. He offered a variety of things available in the kitchen today, and probably also what the family was having. I learned my first lesson about Italian food that evening:

"Fresh is best, and simpler is better."

We had a prawn risotto and mixed grilled vegetables, *risotto con gamberi & insalata verdure miste grigliate*. Eating out of doors really does make everything taste better.

It's a myth that good food has to be complicated. I think the strength and appeal of Italian regional cookery is in plain preparation, which allows the individual flavours to sing. I remember reading from an Italian chef that it is actually incorrect to use onion and garlic in the same dish. I love that. The subtlety of that. Garlic and onion may be interchangeable but using both is gilding the lily.

Our food was simple, fresh, brightly coloured. The risotto was bathed in a delicious passata, which unintentionally complemented the blush of the setting sun. The bread was unsalted, which was traditional, slightly tangy, and chewy.

I looked across the terrace towards the little town, wondering if our new home was waiting for us up there. If we ended up buying a house in Colli, then this hotel could be our "local". How divine. And with an outdoor pool.

The buildings in the village were for the most part made of thick chunky stone, with a pale apricot colour being the most popular. Everything in the village had a genteel, veiled beauty to it, slightly hazy and out of focus. Dream-like. I thought about Bath, and the architectural influences back in England. We were here, at the source of the inspiration.

After dinner, I sat gazing out of the large picture window in the hotel room. The streetlights coiling up the side of the nearby hills were reminiscent of fairy lights, deep golden sodium lights with a pinpoint beam of light. The air was pungent with the scent of valley and hillside plants. Rather incongruously, Bruce Springsteen's *Born in the USA* was playing somewhere far down the valley. The Liri river was long, and any sounds made on the valley floor pinged and resonated up the hillsides and into the thick warm sleepy air. All of the night-time sounds of Italy merged together to form a sort of nocturnal symphony, which lulled me at last to sleep.

I woke with a start, realising that I was in Italy, and it was house hunting day. Sunlight was streaming in the windows. Although the hotel didn't provide room service, when I asked if I could bring our breakfast up to the room to save Peter having to climb stairs, they offered to bring it for me, and I could hear the clink of glasses as they laid out our breakfast things on the first-floor terrace. I peered out of the door, saying my *grazie mille* with confidence. I may have had only a handful of conversational Italian phrases, but I was going to speak these few words with gusto.

The first-floor terrace was opposite our room, and provided views from the same angle as our dinner table the night before, but higher up, and more far reaching. I wished I'd gotten up earlier to swim before breakfast but the long journey had taken its toll and I had slept soundly.

Breakfast was unexpected. There was the same country style bread, plastic wrapped croissants, small packets of melba toast, small packets of *Nutella*, small individual boxes of breakfast cereal, small individual portion jams and jellies, and blood orange flavoured squash. Coffee was served in a metal jug with hot milk. Of greater interest was the fruit bowl. Over the coming two days we were treated to yoghurt, honey, and fresh figs, picked that morning by the owner's father, perfectly ripe.

I wondered how my little fig tree was doing back in springtime Wiltshire. I hoped that one day I would be having my own sun-warmed figs at breakfast.

Soon the appointed time came for Viv and Mario to arrive and pick us up, but there was no sign of them. The taxi driver had experienced difficulty in finding us so I wondered if she was lost, since she was coming from Veroli, about half an hour away. I began ringing her home and work number and got no reply. The sun was so bright, and the pool so inviting. It really was a struggle to keep phoning to arrange to be taken away from this beautiful spot for the whole day.

At last she picked up.

"*Pronto,*" she said, in a broad Australian accent. The phone signal weak and crackling.

"Hi, Viv, is that you?" I said, trying not to show my irritation.

"Yes, hello Marcie, *I'm on my way.*"

No explanation. No apology.

"Uh right, okay, is everything okay?"

"Yes," she snapped. "I'm on my way." She hung up.

My stomach flopped. This was not good.

She hadn't given an estimated arrival time, so we ended up cooling our heels for another forty-five minutes before they finally put in an appearance.

The car was nice, but she was not.

She had a broad face, thin brown hair, little embroidered flat shoes, stylish capri pants. Her husband Mario was Italian, dark skinned, dark hair, strong Roman nose.

"Is everything okay?" I reiterated, hoping for an explanation, some sort of apology.

She stared at me, frozen in her tracks.

"I left my phone at home and had to go back." She defied me to object, and she certainly wasn't going to apologise. "You know, it's very unusual to expect an estate agent to chauffeur clients around to property viewings. You're lucky that we have agreed to do this. The properties you want to see are quite far apart."

I stared back, fish-like.

Peter interjected. "Right, let's have a look at the five properties on our list. The first one – "

She cut him off.

"Yes we've had a look at the ones you've chosen and we think only two of them are really suitable, based on what you told us you were looking for."

I looked across as Mario; he was staring off into the middle distance.

"Erm…" I stammered, "…we really were expecting to see five properties, we've chosen them all very carefully".

I thought she was going to shout at me. Her face flushed.

"These properties are all very far apart! We couldn't possibly see them all in one day and you said you're leaving in the morning for Perugia. There are only two here that are right for you. If you're not happy with it then we'll cancel the whole arrangement!"

I was floored. This was not at all what I'd been expecting. had been so seduced by Italy: the food, the weather, the scenery. To be barked at by an angry Australian was very jarring.

Peter and I looked at each other. There was a very tense moment while we considered whether or not to chuck in the whole plan or put up with her rudeness.

"Okay, whatever, lead the way." I backed down, wilting.

"Fine!" Viv said, turning smartly and striding towards the car, Mario loping behind. She'd won and she knew it. And I knew it. And now I was mad.

We were headed off to Posta Fibreno, a lovely lake and nature reserve in the foothills. I couldn't enjoy the scenery though, I was too uncomfortable wedged in the back next to Viv, fuming. I couldn't figure out why she hadn't recommended more time to view all of the places we wanted. We could have stayed another day, no problem. I was mystified. The men sat up front, rarely speaking. The location was pretty enough, and it would have been wonderful living near a lake, just half a block away.

My heart sank when we arrived. The property could be seen up a flight of steps, through thick undergrowth. We had said we didn't want a fixer-upper. Why were we here? The building looked like an annex for a next-door property, whose common wall was very high and dark. I didn't get a sense that the little house ever saw the light of day.

I always get a buzz off of seeing old fixer-uppers, but we had actually been through all that in Wales, and were old enough now to need something which didn't need massive restoration. It was gloomy and morose inside, not helped by the friction between Viv and myself. One room contained a very graceful staircase, spiralling through a lovely opening in the ceiling. I lost myself for a moment, admiring its grace, but common sense told me that one staircase was not enough to merit buying a liability.

I left in a black mood, but not sufficiently courageous to take on Viv in another sparring match. Our next – and last – house of the day, was back in little Colli. My spirits lifted a bit as I had had such a good feeling about the place during dinner the night before. We parked in a beautiful little square in the centre of town, inlaid with different coloured cobbles marking out the 17th century date of the church.

The entire palazzo was painted in the warm apricot colour I had seen before, gently peeling, cracked and broken in places, giving off the air of a rather dignified elderly lady, aged but noble. The palazzo was a stocky building, not overly ornate. The wrought iron railings had some flair but for the most part the building was serviceable, and big, and old. It was a long narrow building, next door to the church which was in the centre of the town. The palazzo then extended down a little lane, also cobblestoned, and so narrow that you might be tempted to stretch your arms out and see if you could touch both sides at the same time. Viv told us that the building belonged to the noble family of the area, but if it the letter 'p' in the name was lower case then it wasn't a royal family. An upper case 'P' was something special. We didn't mind about the small 'p': we weren't looking for something noble. We wanted light, space and air.

The Italians understand space. How to balance height and depth. How to keep a corridor wide, and a stairwell ceiling high. How rooms can flow into each other through archways and tall narrow ornate French doors.

We trooped down the little lane looking for *numero cinque*, Viv picking her way carefully across the cobbles in her little embroidered flats. Suddenly, there it was: I recognised the door. And my heart exploded.

In front of us was an enormous battle-axe of a door. It looked as if it had been designed to repel Barbarians. Two graceful door knockers – a lady's hand holding a ball – drew the eye upwards. Everywhere else had heavy metal studs and brown metal sheeting. The arch of the door frame had an elaborate – and stained – corbel which served as a keystone. It was heart-stoppingly beautiful.

I forgot my anger, I forgot the other houses, I forgot to be mad at Viv. When I stepped through the immense door into the cool of the gloom inside, I knew I was home.

A tall, vaulted ceiling in the entry hall led the eye across and up an enormous stone staircase towards the bedrooms upstairs. The building was made entirely of stone, with marble floors throughout, doorways and window frames framed in dark wood, thick glass in the windows.

Everything seemed to have been built on a larger-than-life scale; I felt like I was in Alice in Wonderland, so small inside the large house. At the back of the ground floor was a small, incredibly intense room papered with an oxblood red and white intricate design. The pattern looked Baroque. The floor was also richly patterned in a five-colour

Baroque styled ceramic tile design, framed with terracotta. Someone had really gone to town with the pattern and the colour but somehow it worked. Two pairs of dark green metal shutters were opened to reveal the sort of view mostly reserved for movies. I loved this room. It was mad, it was chaotic, it was Italian.

The building was sparsely furnished with some rather dubious, and some frankly appalling furniture, the sort of furniture which is bought in haste in one's youth, and carted around from house to house until age, or an increase in finances, guarantees its demise. The owners now lived in Rome I was told. Perhaps this house had become their second home, and then became the receptacle for unwanted furniture. One or two pieces were quite nice. We were told that some of the furniture was available as part of the purchase, which might be helpful to us, if we could find anything to our taste.

The tall slim French doors in every room were painted a pale sage green, with gilt trim. Overhead in every room were massive, intricate wrought iron chandeliers, like elaborate big black spiders preparing to pounce. They weren't exactly to my taste, but I happily accepted them because they were authentic Italian.

We spoke in hushed tones; the sound pinging off the stone walls exaggerated every syllable. There were two bedrooms and a bathroom upstairs, but what we saw in the sitting room took my breath away: four immense pairs of French doors looking out over the Liri river valley to three aspects. And against the fourth wall, a pink marble fireplace.

It wasn't just pink; it was *Barbie* pink. Ornate. Florid. Whimsical. Flanked by two smirking marble faces. I laughed outright when I saw it. *"I don't think we're in Kansas anymore, Toto..."* I mused inwardly. The room itself was light and incredibly airy, vaulted, painted a pale cream colour. The chandelier in this room was crystal, and the rainbow light winked and flashed into every corner of the room.

The window treatments in each room were incredibly elaborate, and luckily for us, in very good condition. First you opened a pair of internal wooden shutters, designed to keep the light out. Next were thick glass casement windows which opened inwards. Third was a retractable mesh fly screen, which in most rooms was in very good condition. The screens pulled down and locked into place with a spring-loaded mechanism. They were not always reliable and sometimes took on a life of their own. They had been fitted well and at great expense. Lastly were the exterior metal louvre shutters, painted dark green, which opened outwards and welcomed the views below. These shutters were in a more dubious state, being the last bastions before the harsh elements of the Italian weather. They were meant to be held in place with brass clasps attached to the exterior of the house, but for the most part the clasps were broken, or twisted, or limply dangling into space.

I was besotted.

Tall doors opened out onto a modest terrace which faced inwards towards the little lane, devoid of view, but with an appealing roofscape. Even though it was only mid-morning, the terracotta tiles were hot to the touch as they absorbed the heat. I pictured sunny breakfasts and long, lingering suppers out here. Peter was humming happily. As we got our bearings, we noticed that there was another apartment semi-detached from ours but built one storey higher, so this terrace was overlooked by what we assumed was another member of the palazzo's noble family. Opposite us on two sides were other houses, rather close in proximity. Below us there was the vacant unrestored coach house, and also somehow another apartment, tucked away at a sort of angle which I could never really figure out. But from the sitting room, out the window, was a sheer drop down to the valley floor, a sense of space and light which is hard to describe.

Viv took me down to the boiler room, the stairs being steep and precarious and not entirely suited to Peter's limited mobility. It was a boring and acrid little room, neat as a pin, buried deep in the bowels of the vast building. I should have paid more attention to it but I was in the first flushes of young love and wasn't concentrating. I was daydreaming about Italian meals, and parties, and summers spent laughing with my family, just back from a swim in the hotel pool and living life to the full. *La Dolce Vita was within our grasp.*

Viv knew that this house was the one. She wasn't planning to take us on a wild goose chase out to the far reaches of Sora, or Arpino, when this house fulfilled the wildest dreams of any English family abroad. I was still mad at her for being late, and rude, and bolshie, but my anger was diluted somewhat by the awareness that we were at the end of the rainbow here, in Colli.

I barely noticed the coach house. It was a great project, but at that moment was dark, dank, and a poor second cousin to the glorious Queen upstairs. At least it had a lovely bit of terraced garden – unkempt – and those beautiful, vaulted ceilings, but my heart was gone, stolen, imbedded in the thick stone walls upstairs.

Our work was done. Viv knew we were off tomorrow for Perugia, and she knew that she had won the day. It was only a matter of time before we would be back, negotiating, and offering a deposit to secure our glorious little bit of Italy.

A sun-warmed pool feels different from a heated pool. The water feels softer somehow, more comforting. If you paddle your legs in the deep end you can still feel the cooler water which the sun hadn't reached, giving it a sort of complexity.

I swam in the pool of the Ville de Colle hotel and felt at home. I stretched my arms and legs as wide as they would go and revelled in the feeling of being encased in water, wrapped in water, soothed and comforted by water. I could see for miles from that pool, high up as we were on the top of the hill. The sun was setting; the air and sky were changing.

I had fallen in love with a house that afternoon. It was possible to own that house, and live in that house, and maybe swim in this pool. My heart was so full as I swam. I actually felt very Italian: passionate, impulsive, expressive.

Peter and I have a phrase, a secret little phrase between us: a "Pinksmore Moment". He remembered one time, when he was a boy, lying on his back in a field outside Pinksmore, in Somerset. He looked up at the sky, and felt an overwhelming sense of peace. He felt no urgency or ambition or anxiety. He was in precisely the right place at the right time and he felt balance and serenity. Pretty heady stuff, for a young lad. But I knew exactly what that felt like. I had had it too, when being driven at high speed round a windy road in a convertible sports car, with the roof down, driven by someone who really krew what he was doing behind the wheel. The air was racing past me and the car was really eating up the miles but I felt lifted and suspended above the car, free from fear, free from fate.

I had a Pinksmore Moment in the hotel pool at the Ville de Colle. I suddenly understood what my life was about, and my destiny, and it felt good. Yes, we were going to Perugia the next morning, and I was looking forward to that, but more in the sense that we would be exploring another part of my new country, my new home, and I was curious and excited about that. Because I had a pretty good inkling that soon I would be back here in this pool, and I would be calling Colli my home.

BLOG POST: AN ITALIAN MEAL

DINING IN ITALY

What an enormous topic: dining in Italy!

Everyone needs to eat, whether you're a resident or a tourist; it's a basic element of life. But there is something about dining in Italy that can elevate this simple transaction into a thing of beauty: it is the concept of ordering food as a conversation, not an order.

We spent four days at LA VILLE DEL COLLE, just outside Monte San Giovanni Campano, in Lazio. We were having meetings and appointments to finalize the purchase of our new home, so we were in and out dining at the hotel, in cafes, and once a picnic from a deli in Arpino as well.

The manager, Andreas, would arrive at our table in the evening and say "What would you like tonight?" If we knew specifically, we would say, but more often than not he would suggest something that maybe had come in fresh that morning, or was a contrast to what we had had before. He might simply say "Fish? Rice? Pasta?"

It's a bit like casting a play. The agent negotiates the star players, and then the rest of the cast is hired to support the stars. The key words 'rice' or 'fish' would be sent to the kitchen and then the chef would get busy, and something plainly cooked and utterly delicious would appear quite quickly on our plates.

I don't, however, want to give the impression that you can just waltz into any Italian restaurant, anywhere in the country, and start demanding whatever you're in the mood for. Of course it doesn't work that way. If there is a printed menu, then read the menu, and respect the plan that the chef has in store for you. If you have read up on the regional specialities in the area you're visiting, then that arms you with more information on what to expect, and also helps you to avoid items that you might find unappealing.

When I first arrived I stupidly specified salmon, knowing full well that it was likely to be farmed salmon and really not an Italian kind of thing. If I wanted salmon on this occasion, I might just as well have stayed in Wiltshire. By the end of the visit we were completely in the hands of the kitchen, and when we were asked "Fish?" we just said "yes", knowing that it was going to be amazing, and different, and beautifully cooked. Sometimes it was perfectly grilled gamberetti, (a large crustacean), or a delicious terracotta-coloured risotto with a rich tomato-based fish sauce and flakes of fish. The swordfish was new for me: meaty, tender, grilled and presented on a bed of radicchio, next to more gamberetti, and a slice of bream.

Ask for "pollo" and you might get a fresh fillet of boneless chicken breast, pounded flat, plainly grilled, and served with a wedge of lemon. Honestly, if you are travelling with fussy children, I do believe you can banish the word 'nugget' from your vocabulary, as lovely, plainly cooked fresh chicken will be a steady diet for the toddler brigade.

Chicken is seen on menus more often in some regions than in others, Lazio being one of them.

Expect to have, at the very least, two courses, as Italian meals are served à la russe (in courses) as opposed to à la francaise (altogether at one time). Try not to tinker with this method too much, as the composition of ingredients, and the order in which they are presented, is part of the fun, and the artistry, of Italian cuisine. I came in one evening and asked for pasta with grilled vegetables. I was advised to have the pasta course first, and then the main course second, with grilled vegetables as a side dish. Salad as a side will be readily available and can be an insalata mista (mixed green salad with vegetables) or insalata verde (green salad).

When preparing a pasta course, the size and shape of the pasta will be determined by the other ingredients in the dish. If you were going to have a light sauce and a thin angel hair pasta, then big chunky grilled vegetables would weigh it down and spoil the dish. In the autumn, a rich wild boar ragu would need a chunky, substantial pasta shape to support it, and would sit awkwardly on a bowl full of dainty grains of orzo.

A PROPER ITALIAN LUNCH

One day we went out to lunch: a proper Italian lunch.

We were entirely in the hands of our Italian-speaking friends and the chef.

Upon arrival at IL CICLOPE, near Arpino, we were greeted by the sight of a large ramshackle shack, with dubious wooden walls, and mostly taken up inside by a large wood-burning fireplace. A bronzed and elderly gentleman grinned at us as we arrived: he was in charge of grilling. Beneath a thick stone, shelf-like hearth lay his black, portly, ancient labrador, snoozing on her bed under the warmth of the fire.

Our table was close to the indoor kitchen, in a smart yellow building, the doorway hung with the traditional curtain of long plastic beads in order to deter insects. Soon the hostess arrived, and after much hugging and kissing and chatting with our friends, the serious business of ordering began. Lamb was suggested (star player), or maybe pasta (co-star). Pizza is a popular selection for that wood-fired oven, but only in the evenings. 'Pasta with wild mushrooms' was discussed briefly, but maybe not to be ordered in the month of May. Truffle, here, is typical and readily available, fresh and in oil. Its smoky, dense, pungent essence makes a star player out of anything it touches.

As we settled into our seats under the trees, plates appeared with antipasti, the Italian equivalent of hors-d'oeuvres. These were not fiddly little things balancing precariously on melba toast. They were hearty, small-portioned offerings designed to accompany the large glass jugs of red and white wine which descended on our table. Antipasti wake up the taste buds, and focus your attention on the meal at hand. Several at this restaurant were dough-based or with potato. Offerings will be different in other parts of the country. Some were like small cubes of vegetable tarts. There were cubes of sautéed cabbage with ham, and stuffed grilled peppers. We tasted a bowl of crunchy deep-fried dough rings, which are popular at the village fetes which criss-cross the country throughout the year. Cubes of potato cakes were light and fluffy.

It seemed as though the chef, in the kitchen, would send out some offerings, then look in the fridge for inspiration, and then create yet another plate of tasty morsels to be sent out; there must have been about six plates of antipasti in the end, before we headed onto our main.

A large platter of green salad sailed in, fresh and lightly dressed. A bowl filled with slices of the local bread, chewy and dense, was wrapped in a clean cloth.

The pasta course, a beef ragu on a bed of wide noodles (pappardelle) was rich, pungent, and fresh, served with a long-stemmed glass heaped high with grated Pecorino Romano. We were all completely full after only two courses, and yet still managed to squeeze in a generous dollop of tiramisu, and several small glasses of cherry ratafia, before we reluctantly piled into cars and drifted off.

Everybody you meet in Italy seems to know about, and understand, food, and be interested in what is being served. In many countries, music and sport bring people together. In Italy, I would add food to the list. An appreciation of the joy of cuisine, and seasonal food, and sharing a meal with friends, gives a connection to others, and a connection to the earth, which is a truly life-enhancing element of la dolce vita.

Dinner that night was plain and perfect: Linguine con funghi followed by scaloppine di pollo in lightly seasoned flour, with a lemon wedge. Always a bit of salad, always the local tangy bread. My muscles felt relaxed and soothed by the swim, and the warm dry air embraced us.

Little Georgio was beginning to get used to us, peeping shyly out from the door of the hall up towards our table. He would giggle and disappear if he was spotted.

I realised I could see our house from the terrace, from our actual table, seeing exterior parts of it from the hotel which we hadn't seen during the visit. The roof was a fairly shallow pitch, tiled, and in very good condition. I could see the banks of green shutters marching around the exterior: so many windows, so many shutters, so much light pouring into that house. The sheerness of the drop into the valley below was accentuated. The house blended into other houses up and down the tiny street because of its faded apricot colour, and yet the house also stood out from its neighbours because of its handsomeness.

I slept well that night.

The morning light caught us out. I leapt out of bed and had a swim before breakfast, feeling the difference between the pool's evening water and its morning water. The light came from a different direction in the morning, lighting everything around the pool but not the pool itself until later in the day. So the air felt slightly cooler than the water, making the pool water more comforting than the air around it.

We said our goodbyes to Andreas and his family, leaving in a taxi for the rail station with my handbag stuffed full of single portion Nutella packets (for travel emergencies).

Our driver was a tiny, pert, slightly madcap woman named Graziella. She had a slightly 1950's flair about her, as if she had just finished filming a dance sequence from *Ready Steady Go!* She handled the mountain roads of Lazio like an expert, driving confidently with one hand, using the other to gesticulate, or ring her daughter, or scrabble round for something in the glovebox. She had no English to speak of whatsoever, which made the free hand all the more important, as it helped her to mime words she could not say.

She guided us directly to the train platform, ensured we got on, waved us off cheerily with the expression of one who knew that we were smitten kittens, and soon to be back in our newfound home.

By this time I had done some research about Rome, and I was very anxious. Bloggers, mostly women, trumpeted warnings about thieves, pickpockets, dubious shadowy Italians lurking in corners. I remembered the cellophane wrapped suitcases in the airport, and I hugged my luggage closely to me. Apparently, Roma Termini was the worst. You were advised not to speak to anyone or be distracted from your journey. If someone approached you and offered to help you, they would suddenly turn on you and demand money for their service. Perhaps they might just steal your wallet, or your handbag, while you were trying to find out which platform you needed. Maybe you would be targeted for a mugging, down a dark alley. The taxi you climbed into could rip you off if it didn't have a little white sign on the roof, establishing that it was a legitimate service vehicle. The driver might take you round the long way to your destination, or try coercing you into creepy hotels which they knew, and had shady dealings with.

I longed for the pool and the house, and the *affogato al caffe* at the hotel. Peter was encouraging me to try some of the excellent cafes and food stalls at Termini but I was frightened and didn't want to appear to be lost or hanging around. I had my *Nutella* packets for emergencies, remember.

We found our connection to Spoleto and collapsed gratefully into our seats, breathing a sigh of relief. My hands ached from gripping my luggage too tightly. Today was only a travel day, as Peter had scheduled our visits with Giada the day afterwards, so I sat back mesmerised by the scenery playing out before me.

Our hotel in Spoleto faced onto the main piazza, and I could watch the local Italians playing out their afternoon lives from our little hotel room balcony. It looked a very pleasant town; its music festival was world renowned. Dinner that night was in a pocket-sized restaurant, *Cinque Cente*. Slim Italian girls fluttered around huge communal platters of food, gossiping, and then adjourned outside to smoke. They didn't just pick at the food, pretending to be on diets, in the American fashion; they dived in and ate heartily, and somehow it never showed an ounce on their hips or their waistlines.

My black rice and pumpkin starter looked beautiful enough to be in an exhibition, moulded with a film of gelatine into a tidy little tower. The contrast between the deep black wild rice grains and the brilliant orange pumpkin seemed to stop all conversation in the room. The best Italian food was still the simplest, and this was too; they just used colour to take it to that higher level. Wild rice and pumpkin. Delicious, nutritious, Italian.

The proprietor sauntered around the room, chatting to friends, discussing the menu, overseeing the staff with a relaxed informality and authority. It could for all the world be a dinner party in his own home. We wished that this restaurant could be our local too, but we were now hours from little Colli and its hilltop hotel. Music and chocolate, music and chocolate, I went to sleep dreaming of the two memorable products of Perugia, beautiful things which make life worth living.

I woke the next morning with mixed feelings. I was very excited about seeing the properties here, and slightly worried that I would see something that would take my heart away from Colli. If that was what happened, then wonderful, we would be living in this beautiful place, where to be honest English was more frequently used, and our chocolate and music-filled lives would be very happy. Spoleto had more creature comforts. The buildings seemed more stylish and not quite so rustic.

Meeting Giada was like meeting a whirlwind of long flowing hair and smiles. She was a tall, willowy, woman, such a welcome change from controlling little Viv. It was true, it wasn't normally an estate agent's job to ferry us around but she had agreed without hesitation, escorting us to her car with a smile. We climbed quickly towards Perugia and to the little town of Piegaro, high up in the surrounding hills. She was an excellent ambassador for *Festival dei Due Monde*, having worked there herself. She'd had such an exciting life, formerly a dancer with Martha Graham, and was such a vibrant example of Spoleto life. What happened next became one of the first posts on my then new blogsite: *www.italyfoodtraveller.blogspot.com*.

BLOG POST: GENTLEMEN

It wasn't particularly hot by Italian standards, but the Volvo just couldn't take it any longer. Giada, our estate agent, spends a lot of her working day on the road and maintains the car well, but she had never been to this house before, and even she was struck by the steepness of the road, the heat of the day, and the remoteness of the property.

We were having a lively conversation about ballet (she is a former professional dancer with the esteemed Martha Graham dance troupe). Suddenly, the dials on the dashboard went haywire, and things began to flash.

Muttering under her breath in a mixture of English and Italian, Giada managed to haul the big metal hulk across somewhat near the side of the road. Insidious steam and smoke began whisping from under the bonnet. Something was very wrong with this car.

Amazingly, Giada had a phone signal, and she immediately rang Casaitalia International Real Estate for help. I got out of the car and wandered over to the edge of the road, taking in the glorious views over Perugia, wavering and shimmering in the heat. I decided to make friends with this view and this road; it looked like we were going to be here a while. I admired Giada's energy and positive attitude. She spoke with equal confidence in English and Italian, and with great energy about a wide variety of topics, covering property, geography, art, music, dance, politics, and food. I could tell already that this was not going to be just any old property viewing.

Casaitalia International Real Estate (www.casait.it) offers premiere properties for sale throughout Italy. Many of their property listings are the stuff of dreams, of glossy magazines, and of the exclusive, privileged few. The villa we were on our way to visit was an exquisite chocolate box of a holiday villa, part of an exclusive little commune. It was beautifully frescoed and balconied, deep in the hills, with a large, sunny shared swimming pool. It looked incredible in the brochure, but we were nowhere near the house; we were halfway up a very remote and dusty road, feeling the heat and trying not to worry.

A white van appeared on the horizon; I couldn't believe it. Before we could raise a hand to flag it down, the van pulled over and two electricians got out. A lot of Italian ensued. There were gestures, and smiles, and a bit of head nodding, and even more Italian. I didn't know where these men were headed but it didn't seem to matter to them; they just dropped whatever they were doing to help us. They just changed gears and helped us.

Up came the car bonnet, and one of the men gingerly covered his hand with a shirt sleeve and tested the radiator cap. He snatched his hand back quickly, took off his company jacket, and with a guffaw, began to unscrew the radiator cap with all the delicacy of a bomb *disposal expert.*

I plugged my ears. I don't know why. The second man hovered, and Italianated.

Giada took sips from a large bottle of water, and rang the caretaker, who we were due to meet at the villa. She was what the English would describe as 'grace under pressure.' She was utterly charming to the men, but without playing the helpless female role. She never lost her cool, and was always professional and on top of things. But there was such a sense of fun about her, amidst all of this chaos, and the men just adored it.

More Italian ensued. The two men peered suspiciously under the bonnet, as boiling liquid, a disturbing shade of magenta, began to erupt over the radiator and down onto the road.

I stood there, staring, a packet of chocolate biscuits melting quietly in the palm of my hand. My husband leaned against the car, amused, just taking it all in.

By now there was a quite a lot of Italian being spoken, simultan-eously, and there was a somewhat festive air about the proceedings. The men chuckled, Giada gestured down the phone, I passed around the sticky bickies. My husband squinted up at the midday sun.

Amazingly, yet another car appeared over the brow of the hill: it was the caretaker. Giada smiled, and waved, and laughed, and we all greeted him with the bonhomie of long-lost soldiers. He returned our smiles, and approached the stricken vehicle with an air of authority. I could tell he was a man who was used to sorting things out. He proceeded to top up the radiator with even more water, carefully poised over the engine like a surgeon.

By now there was just so much Italian being spoken. The men were delighted with their roles as heroes, and we felt so secure and cared for, in our helpless condition, and more help was being promised down the phone. The sun was blazing, spirits were high, and I just thought: "Oh Italia! What a glorious place to be rescued in!" People here just notice, and help, and chip in. It's not a courtesy thing; it's just a sort of human nature sort of thing, a quality of caring that I don't see very often.

We had a similar experience at the airport in Rome. We had arranged for airport assistance at Fiumencino airport, from our *EasyJet* flight. My husband, who has difficulty walking long distances, required a wheelchair. We were duly met by an airport attendant, a kindly, burly young man with shoulder-length corkscrew curls. We extended our limited Italian greetings and began to move down the corridor, when he suddenly excused himself, in broken English, and gestured for us to stay where we were. He moved off in the direction of the other disembarking passengers, and I began to panic. The last time we had been left by an airport attendant, in LAX, we were abandoned by the wheelchair attendant in front of a lift and he never returned.

Determined not to be a victim again, I struggled on our way, weaving slightly under the weight of two suitcases, two carry-on bags, and the wheelchair. After a few hundred feet I looked back and saw the young airport attendant, belting towards us with an indignant look on his face. Through gestures and limited English he made us aware that he was coming back, he was planning to help us, and I had no business driving his chair!

He took great pride in his official airport uniform, and his badge, and the privileges it gave him. We swanned past long queues of passengers, and down corridors reserved for airport staff. He greeted the Passport Control attendant like a friend, and chatted amiably (probably about the football) while handing over our passports and flight details. He asked us where we needed to go, and took us directly to the train station to meet our connection to Rome Termini. He treated my husband with such respect, and treated me rather like an insolent puppy, caught smuggling a bedroom slipper into its dog bed.

Again, I had the sense of someone who wasn't necessarily instructed to be courteous; he just saw what needed to be done and did it, went the extra mile to do the job well.

Back to our car. We managed to cajole the car up the hill and across to the shade of the villa complex. Mr. Adolfo Giovannelli, CEO of Casaitalia, arrived in person and gave us his own car, to ensure our safe arrival back *at our hotel. I'm not sure what happened to him. We left him at the villa, in the quavering heat of the afternoon sun, abandoned with our poorly car in the shade of an olive tree, chatting amiably to the caretaker.*

What a gentleman. They were all such gentlemen. In the heat, and the dust, and the annoyance of things breaking down, we were surrounded by everyday gentlemen making life just that little bit more lovely.

We didn't take the house, as it happened. It was a house for rest, and for play, and for falling off the grid for a bit. I was looking for a launchpad for my new life. But I feel we have made new friends and forged a lasting respect for the considerate citizens of Italy who we have come across on our travels.

The villa was an absolute delight. It was part of a little commune of semi-detached former farm-workers cottages, high up in the Perugian hills, in the middle of nowhere. The current owner must have loved the little house very much; it was decorated with lovely little hand-painted frescoes. We had seen a few of these little communes listed on Rightmove, small ones and two-bedroom units with shared grounds and a shared pool. It was a wonderful idea for people who wanted either a little bolthole, or a holiday lettings business. The pool stood a bit further away from the property, laid out in a wide flat section of the grounds and, on this day in particular, looked very enticing. The communal grounds were managed by a property group; they and the properties looked immaculately maintained, and for a second home it would be ideal. I adored the small–scale frescoes and the building itself, but I had a fixed belief that we needed to be walking distance to shops and services, and that driving was going to be challenging, so we decided not to pursue it.

The last property we visited was made memorable by the fact that the owner tried to peer up my skirt as I climbed the wrought iron staircase in his lounge. Despite the benefit of a lovely deep shady terrace, and its superb location near Spoleto, my heart still lay in Colli, and couldn't be dislodged.

We boarded the train in Spoleto, having given fond farewells to Giada. I felt sure we would meet each other again one day, probably at the festival. Our train took us straight into Rome Termini.

Our Rome hotel was near the airport. I lay on the bed that night, exhausted but with my mind racing. I had so much of everything in the past few days: sunshine, amazing food, colour, culture, light, space, air, water, old houses, new houses. I couldn't believe this was our life: actually planning to move to Italy. It wasn't a dream, it was really doable, and we were going to do it very soon.

The vague ideas about my career began to fall into place. I could cater, write about food, learn about food, maybe run a little cookery school. Living outside of Rome part of the year, and also outside of Bath, seemed to make absolute sense. I felt enormously content as we boarded the airplane for Bristol. My muscles were warm and relaxed from the sun, and I felt so healthy from the nutritious and delicious food I'd been eating for the past four days. The pieces of the puzzle were nearly all in place.

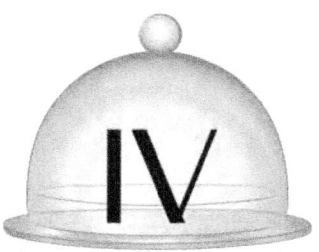

What Happened Next

We weren't terribly thrilled about doing any further business with Viv and Mario, but they were the gatekeepers to our dream house so we decided to grin and bear it. I hadn't realised that there were so many differences between Italy and England as regards the law, and the process of buying a house. We had no contacts whatsoever in Italy, so whatever searches or document preparation we needed invariably ended up going through the estate agents. We were conscious of the fact that, were they the sort of people to be unscrupulous, we could be taken advantage of, but we had few alternatives. I had contacted *Italy Property Guide* to find a recommended Italian solicitor, but he was based in Milan and didn't have any local connections to refer us to for negotiating the deal.

We asked for a structural survey and Viv provided a *geometra*, or *surveyor*, who gave us a rather cursory report of one and a half pages, claiming that the property was sound and habitable, describing things about the building that were already obvious to the naked eye. We assumed that for the price we were paying the structural survey would include testing water and electrics but apparently this was extra.

We were told that many people wanted a *Certificate of Habitability* to certify that the property was safe to live in. Mario suggested that this was not mandatory and would cause further delay, and costs. My house was under offer in Anglesey, so we knew exactly how much money we were going to have available to us; it was going to be tight. We also wanted some of the nicer pieces of furniture still left in the house, so at least we had a bed or two to sleep on when we arrived, and some cupboards.

I am a very impatient and impulsive creature, qualities not best suited to the purchase of foreign property. Peter is wiser and more phlegmatic, but even he was getting fed up with the annoying emails and double speak emerging from Viv's office. We both just wanted to have done with it, and we decided we'd sort whatever needed sorting after the purchase had been completed.

We arranged a second flying visit to Lazio in order to sign the paperwork and exchange. We were now going to meet the owners, who were very vivid in my imagination. Back to the Ville del Colle we went, arranging transport from Graziella, and looking forward to hopefully another Pinksmore Moment in the swimming pool.

Lucio and Antoinetta were a dignified couple. He was wider than he was tall, and far more interested in having a beer with us at the wide oak table in the dining room, than negotiating about the house. She was slim, birdlike, gracious. She offered us espresso instead, in tiny china cups, accompanied by thin pink wafer biscuits. Neither of them had a word of English, so we had our mime skills at the ready.

An estate agent from Rome was also in attendance, hovering in the background and quietly muttering to Viv and Mario behind our backs. Lucio was a retired doctor and had once been held in high esteem in the village. They now lived in air-conditioned comfort, in Rome.

I have the annoying habit of becoming very ingratiating with strangers. I found it a challenge to balance this feeling with the blatant disregard I felt for Viv and Mario. Antoinetta showed us around, telling us interesting little tidbits about the house and the furniture, which she was keen to sell as well. She nearly convinced me to buy a very large human- sized floor cushion in white silk with gold braid and tassles. She draped herself carefully on the cushion and struck a pose for me, with a little twinkle in her eye. I think it was her favourite spot in the house, positioned as it was on the floor between the cooling breezes of two pairs of open French doors. I'd earmarked that particular spot for a little breakfast table in what was to be our bedroom, so resisted the temptation.

Behind the scenes, things were getting stressy. The bridging loan we had acquired from our Anglesey beach house to buy the restaurant in Wiltshire was now used as the deposit to buy the Colli house. But we needed to complete on the Anglesey sale before we could complete on Colli. I had the oddly mixed feelings of wanting to rush things and get to Italy asap, and trying to stall things so that the sale on our beach house could be completed.

August was a nightmare. Everybody started going on holiday, and in Italy everybody goes at the same time, for a fortnight. The whole country shuts down. Nobody is concerned about delicate negotiations, or completion dates. Everybody just chills.

It was driving me wild.

Lucio and Antoinetta disappeared at one point, after we paid the deposit, and I began to panic that we would never see them again. Viv and Mario were planning to go to Venice. There was absolutely no chance of getting any work done in August, before we moved in, so we had to resign ourselves to the prospect of living there while decorating was going on. Two deadlines for completion came and went, and the delays were on our side. If there wasn't a history of heart attacks in my family already, I was about to be the first.

At last, the beach house was sold. After one final flying visit, one final meal at the hotel, one final dip in the pool, we met for the exchange of contracts and keys. Lucio looked grim. No one was interested in having a beer on this occasion, sat as we were in the office of the notary. Thing were said in Italian. The men looked grim and business-like. Lucio began to perspire in his heavy suit jacket. He had a curious, almost guilty look on his face as he handed over the keys. I wasn't sure what that was all about but I clocked it, and it worried me.

The keys were finally ours. A huge ring of them, about ten all told. Big chunky keys, slightly rusted, small-sized modern shiny keys, boring but important middle-sized keys, each with a little laminate tag labelling them, in Italian. I carried them carefully to the rental car like gifts of the Magi. My imagination was running wild, picturing us at last in our own little slice of Italy.

Then the fun started. Fun of a different sort.

BLOG POST: THE ITALIAN ADVENTURE BEGINS

"DON'T KEEP CAMPARI IN THE FRIDGE."

It was a gentle reprimand, and I could see a twinkle in my husband's eye as he passed me, sailing out of the kitchen waving an icy glass filled with Campari and Sicilian blood orange juice.

Neither of us really could be cross today, because today, after an agonizing wait, our offer had been accepted on a magical new home in Italy: the wing of a 17th century palazzo.

The phone call came just as I stepped out of the shower. I had a tension headache from the stress of waiting all day, and I was dripping profusely when I grabbed my mobile, which I had put at arm's length outside the shower stall. There was excited squealing on the other end of the line, cut up with line interference on this international call. Our estate agent had just been on a nightmare journey to Venice for her birthday and had been stuck in a rail tunnel for ages with low battery and no air con. She had now arrived at her birthday destination, and was greeted with gondolas and a commission on my house purchase.

My habit of refrigerating everything comes from a childhood upbringing in Southern California, where long hot summers meant melted butter, and ants, and sticky chocolate chip cookies in the cookie jar. My husband, having been raised in Kent and also the West Country, was used to war-time economy, Bakelite, and limited space in the icebox.

ABOUT ME

I am a caterer and food writer. I will divide my time between our new Lazio home, and Wiltshire, in England. My business www.moveablefeastcateringcompany.com, is now just that. I write, and cook, in two countries.

I'd like to say that my culinary influences include such luminaries as Gordon Ramsay and Heston Blumenthal, but in fact, I have been most affected by firstly, my natural impatience, and secondly, raising my two sons, who are fussy eaters.

I'm not terribly interested in complex sauces and elaborate 12-step recipes. I love to buy great quality ingredients and dress them as simply as possible, to let the natural flavours shine through. This is entirely in step with Italian cuisine, which is probably what draws me to it time and time again. I just love it when a great steak, or roast, or pasta appears, and the flavours just 'ping' on your tongue, and you can tell exactly what's in the preparation, but that in no way diminishes from the sheer magic of the dish.

My family used to play a game in the car: "Where shall we go on our holidays?"

> DAD: Well, I've always wanted to go to Australia.
> ELDEST SON: Ummmm......
> YOUNGEST SON: I like pancakes. We should go to Portugal.
> DAD: Pancakes aren't really a national dish in Portugal, sweetheart, that was an international hotel we were staying at.
> YOUNGEST SON: PANCAKES!!! PORTUGAL!!!
> ME (always): Italy.

ITALIAN REGIONAL CUISINE

We've been to Italy about eight times now, all over the country, and no two trips have been the same. I hear this a lot about the country, that each region is incredibly diverse, and impacted by very different influences. Apart from gelato, which seems to be a national treasure, the chunky unsalted breads of Tuscany seem worlds apart from the silky risottos of Pisa, the thirst-quenching lemons of Amalfi, and the subtle richness of truffles in Lazio.

Before air-miles became a political and ecological issue I used to love to cook with exotic ingredients from far-flung countries. Now I abide by the common-sense theory that: "Foods that grow together taste best together". I know that sounds incredibly simplistic but it's actually true. The melting richness of a Caprese salad confirms that the freshest basil, the plumpest plum tomatoes, and the greenest extra virgin olive oil are enhanced with the softness of local mozzarella from the Milk Mountain region of Amalfi and Campagnia.

THE JOURNEY

And so our journey begins: we are buying a new home in Italy, and then writing and dining our way across the country. When we're in the U.K. I'll be offering courses on my culinary cooking and Italian travels. Follow us for more news and views about Italy and its cuisines.

Ciao!

The Move

In retrospect, we must have been out of our tiny minds, planning an adventure like this.

We weren't talking holiday measures, like a time share on the Costa del Sol or something. This was a Big Deal, the Whole Enchilada, the Mother of All House Moves.

Peter was 79. I was 58. He was retired. I was struggling to find my place in the world. Our boys were young men and setting out to find themselves in life. Our dog was fifteen years old, deaf, blind, on a soft-food diet. We believed that Italy was the logical next step.

Finances were already a problem. The house purchase had eaten up all of the proceeds of the beach house sale, and then some. Peter's pension plus a retirement package from his business meant that we were on a fixed income each month, with very little wriggle room for surprises. We knew that the cost of living in rural Lazio would be far less than the cost of living in Wiltshire, so we had that to look forward to. If we could afford to get there.

We told ourselves that we were moving for health reasons: more sunshine, better weather, fresh healthy food. The drier conditions would help ease Peter's arthritis, and my asthma. Even our dog would benefit. And through my food and travel writing, and (maybe) my cookery school, I would benefit others by showing them healthier ways to live, eat and travel.

It was all good.

I'm not, by nature, a very trusting person, but because of the distances involved, and the lack of Italian, we elected in the end to put our faith and trust in Viv and Mario. We really didn't have much choice. They were well connected in Lazio and had access to everything we needed. We really had to throw ourselves on their mercy and trust that they would help us with the transition.

I spoke with Viv on the phone. It was an odd conversation.

"We're going to move to Colli," I said. "Permanently. We're coming across in September. We'd be really grateful if you could help us get set up."

There was a pause on the other end of the line.

"Oh," said Viv.

"Hello?" I said, after a beat. "Viv? Are you there?"

"I thought you were going to be here only part of the year. Half and half. Maybe let the house when you weren't here." She sounded irritated.

"Uh, well, no, we've decided to make the move permanent. We need a bolthole of some sort, somewhere in the UK, for when we visit the kids, but mostly they'll be coming to us during school holidays. We still have a cottage in North Wales."

"Well, I thought you would want us to manage your property for you while you were in England, and we would organize holiday lettings for you, manage the property, sort your bills, that sort of thing."

"No. Thank you."

Another beat.

"Fine, well, whatever, just let me know when you arrive." She didn't quite slam down the phone, but I could tell she wanted to.

I was mystified. Why would this be annoying for her? I didn't really give it a second thought; I had too many other things to do.

We got some quotes from professional international hauliers, but the prices were way beyond our retirement budget, so we did the next best thing: self- drive.

Tim, the chap who used to do our garden in Wales, had moved

his parents to Spain, and he made it sound so easy. So we asked him. He was an amiable young guy, relaxed and kindly. His wife Debbie, hard as nails, ran a nail bar. He didn't have a license to drive one of those really big lorries, so we proposed that he make two trips to Italy in a smaller van which he could drive. We figured out what we could afford and made him an offer. He decided to bring his mate Tom along, driving through the night, taking it in turns to save money.

The simpler I tried to make everything though, the more complicated things got. We bought a super little second hand 4x4, which was left-hand drive. We mapped out a drive from Wiltshire to Lazio over several days, which would include the two of us, our youngest boy Glyn, our dog, and a small collection of first week essentials. We were motivated by yet another blissful stay at the Ville del Colle and its therapeutic pool.

Once we had arrived in Colli, Tim and Tom would set off from North Wales, in the van rental. They would clear half of the contents of the Wiltshire house and bring it across. They themselves didn't do packing – what with being gardeners and all – so we hired a local Wiltshire firm to come in and do a "Pack Only" job. They would load up, travel to Italy via the Channel Tunnel, drop off in Colli, return to Wiltshire, and bring the remainder of the house contents in a second trip. We would then have our Wiltshire cleaner do a final house deep clean and lock up for us. We were putting an incredible amount of faith in people to do things for us from abroad.

I started to get a little obsessional about the packing. I got multi-coloured sticky notes, and a pen, and went around the house colour-keying everything I could find. Things we wanted moved straight away I would mark with a pink sticky note labelled "Italy 1". Things to come on the second trip would be marked with a green sticky note, "Italy 2." Some things we didn't want to bring at all, but thought our boys might want to inherit someday, were marked with a blue sticky note, "Welsh Cottage". I felt like Monica Geller in the tv show *Friends*.

We had to guess at some things. Like the size of the van and how much we thought it could hold.

This was our fatal flaw.

We hired an excellent team of packers and booked them to prepare our items for an international road trip. Packing household goods properly takes time, and space, and a lot of packing material, which meant that the packed boxes would take up quite a lot of room in the van. It would be difficult to gauge just how much room. They were really professional, and I knew they would do a good job.

Meanwhile, Peter sat down with the enormous family atlas on the kitchen table and planned a route for us through the Channel Tunnel, down through France, staying with a friend in Menton, and then carrying on into Italy. We were planning to stay in the Ville del Colle until our goods arrived, and because we were now a larger party, and included a dog, they booked us into their charming little *casita*, a two bedroomed self-catering cottage in the grounds.

I was so excited I could barely sleep. I was perennially exhausted, couldn't concentrate, was supremely organized, and constantly flustered. *This was our life now. This was really our life.* We were going to be those people who you hear about sometimes who go off and do something daring like move to another country *just because they want to*, and they don't just talk about it, they really go ahead and do it. That was us. We were doing it.

The Arrival

We had the keys. We had the house. Now all we needed was our stuff.

Our drive from England had been long, but exciting, and we were now happily settled into the casita. It was quite near the pool, so swimming twice a day became the norm. All we had to do was be patient until Tim and Tom hauled up into the village in their hired van, and the first of our contents could be unloaded into our new home.

The weather was pretty hot by my standards – dipping in and out of the 30s each day – but we slowed down the pace of our lives and enjoyed ourselves, just waiting, waiting for the van. Lovely views, great food; it was the perfect antidote to the stresses of moving abroad.

We'd had a few reports from Tim; things were not going well. The cigarette lighter in the van was broken, and as this was the source of power for Tim's phone, he was constantly struggling to charge his phone. Even though he had been given an advance, he was mysteriously short of money. Despite our warnings, he had not pre-booked his place on the Eurostar, which cost him significantly more. Sometimes I wondered if perhaps Hard-as-Nails had held some back, but if that were true it was never admitted to. Where had all the money gone? It was a mystery.

We had managed to extricate some explanations from the two men, but not much. They had heard somewhere that by taking clever little side routes you could avoid the Autostrada tolls, and perhaps some of the French tolls as well, so they had ended up in this German route in order to save money. I would've thought that the extra mileage would've negated any savings they might have made, but I didn't say anything. They then said that they didn't pre-book on Eurostar because they weren't sure how to time their arrival. They would have to pre-book, load up the boxes, and travel from Wiltshire down to Kent in order to catch the Eurostar and they didn't want to book something and then not make the departure time. I guess this makes sense; but surely other people do it all the time?

They were barely able to load half of our packed contents into the van. The moving company's packers had been true to their word and packed our belongings extremely thoroughly. We had given notice on our Wiltshire house but it was still quite full of other things of ours. Tim was scheduled to go back for the second load but he wasn't convinced that the van would hold it all.

The nights in the little casita were very hot. We tried leaving the windows open, pulling down the insect screens to keep out the mosquitoes, but somehow the little buggers got in anyway. Nightly we were eaten alive, Glyn in particular. You could hear them, buzzing around your ears just as you were drifting off, and if that didn't wake you, then the sound of someone else in the house slapping away would wake you instead. We had to choose, eventually, between being cooler and eaten alive, or suffocating with the windows shut but avoiding new bites.

There didn't appear to be anyone else staying in the hotel, apart from Andreas' family. Huge breakfast trays were brought down to the room each morning, with the same single-serving packeted continental breakfast items we had had before. The fresh figs and yoghurt were perfect. Occasionally fresh melon might appear, or a plate of cured meats.

Glyn played his guitar, Peter read, I swam a lot, and gazed idly at the stunning views from a patio chair.

We were in a sort of limbo, eager to move in, but enjoying the holiday atmosphere of life in the little house. Whenever I began to stress, I would head for the pool. Tim got a message through that he had gone a different route. He mentioned something about Germany – which was alarming – but Peter assured me that there was a route which could possibly take you across parts of southern Germany before you crossed through the Alps and down into Italy itself. He seemed to constantly run out of cash. We in turn had difficulty in accessing funds from our brand-new Italian bank account, so when Tim asked us for more money we found we were short as well. We had purchased a new cheap Italian phone – a condition of opening the bank account – but it didn't work. I could feel myself winding tightly, so… back to the pool, relax, then head for the shower and more insect repellent.

The valley at night was very animated: a distant sound of American pop music, night birds, laughter and the clink of glasses, dogs barking at nothing in particular, cicadas. We hung our wet swim costumes to dry, on the handles of the heavy front doors, a wonderfully incongruous mix of wrought iron and nylon. Once or twice Glyn and I wandered up the lane towards the new house, but the intense heat made our journey slow and arduous, and eventually we gave up.

Waiting, waiting.

At last! The call we had been waiting for! They were somewhere near Rome and would be with us later on in the day. They were short of money. Again. We couldn't extract anything from our new bank account so Tim borrowed something off his brother back in the U.K. The petrol had been more expensive, the autostrada tolls were unexpectedly frequent. I'm not sure exactly where the money kept going, but it kept going fast. We became anxious about checking out of the hotel because we would then be presented with a bill, and we weren't sure how we could pay it if our bank account wasn't open.

Back to the pool, glass of wine, have a nap, spray on insect repellent. Keep calm, keep cool. The gentle guitar sounds emanating from Glyn's bedroom were more soothing than any balm.

They were due to be with us late afternoon. We finally did check out of the hotel, Peter having paid the bill with an English debit card not the Italian account. We drove up to our new house, unlocked the ancient creaking door, and prepared for the arrival of the van. We hauled in our personal belongings from the hotel and dumped them on the floor. Having bought a few beds with the house purchase, we flopped down on each of them, on the bare mattresses, trying to stay cool, trying to stay calm.

Afternoon came and went. No van. Night was falling. No van. Went back to the hotel for supper, and then back to the house. No van.

Finally, Peter got a crackling, almost indecipherable call from Tim. He was lost. He might be somewhere near us but wasn't sure. Peter began shouting instructions down the phone.

"Can you see a tall wall?"

"A what?"

"A. Tall. Wall. It's the monastery. Very high walls. You can't miss it. It'll be on your right as you go by."

"I can see some houses and some bushes."

"Oh great, that's helpful. Italy's full of houses and bushes."

The line went dead.

Peter rang back.

"What colour is the van?"

"What?"

"Van colour? What colour is the van?"

"White", Tim bellowed.

"Great", Peter muttered, "Every van in Italy is white". He suddenly sat upright, a determined look on his face. "We're going out to look for you," he announced down the phone.

"What? I'm out of money!"

Peter hung up.

We bundled into the car and began to scan the surrounding streets of Colli, unfamiliar though they were, dimly lit by the amber glow of sodium lighting, and slightly unnerving in the dark. We crawled round hairpin bends, up steep hills, help our breath and tried to squeeze the 4x4 down tiny narrow lanes not built for motor vehicles.

We realised that we were unlikely to find them if both of us were moving at the same time, so Peter rang once more and insisted that the van be parked, and that they should just *stay there until we found them*.

To this day I'm not sure how we found them. Probably just chance; Colli's not that big. But by the time we got to the house it was nearly ten o'clock at night, hardly the best time to be unloading a van full of household goods and furniture.

Tim and Tom were absolutely wrecked. Exhausted. And they had only just begun to offload furniture. There was a brief discussion about leaving it until the morning, but after a late, dried-out supper, everyone agreed to just get it done. Tim had a sort of harrowed look in his eyes: the look of a young man who had seen too much. Tom was – well – Tom looked like someone who was the best friend of someone who had seen too much, and had had to hear about it, in the van, all the way from Wiltshire to Lazio. Via Germany.

Everyone tried to be as quiet as possible – it was not the best time to meet the new neighbours – but every little noise bounced off the walls of the tiny little lane and exaggerated itself into something much louder. I felt sure that everybody in the village was now wide awake, listening, hating us, plotting their revenge.

I had stomach problems. I was about to say mercifully, as the unloading was not fun, but I was in my own little mini-drama upstairs, either in the toilet or sprawled on the bed, exhausted, listening to the boxes being carted in down below. There were so many things I was upset about I couldn't even begin to sort them all out. The only decision I could manage to make was whether or not to lurch into the toilet again, or stay collapsed on the bed and wait for the moment to pass.

I fell asleep for a while, and when I woke up it was dark out and everything was quiet. Either the neighbours had executed everyone or the move was over. I staggered downstairs, seeing a sorry group of sweaty disenchanted people sitting at the dining table nursing their beers. Even Glyn looked despondent, and he was normally a stalwart. I tried to mumble something about diarrhoea but decided that no one wanted to hear about it, so I was brief.

"Everybody O.K.?"

"Yes. We're done." They all looked at the floor as they spoke.

"Liars", I thought to myself. "You all hate me and think I pulled a sickie. You're all mad at me."

I tried to behave like someone who had just been through a medical emergency. I tried to imagine how that might look. Then I realised I didn't have to pretend to look like someone who had been very, very ill. *I had been very very ill.* I just had to stand there and let my seaty brow, ashen coloured face, and hunched shoulders do the talking for me.

Somehow the five of us managed to crawl into our makeshift little beds, mostly mattresses on the floor. I took Sandy out for her late-night puddle – for the first time since we'd moved in – but she didn't like doing her business on the pavement so I staggered down the little street, what seemed like miles, until she gave up looking for a park or grassy hill, and crouched in the shadows.

We knew the house and the village by day, but this was our first night here. We overlooked the beautiful river valley. Its steep sides acted as a sort of megaphone for the sounds of the valley at rest. It was not asleep; it was very much alive. The music had stopped, replaced by a different type of music.

For every animal that is active by day, there must be a corresponding animal which flourishes in the dark. I heard strange bird calls, a low nicker from the horses stabled below us, a borec dog barking aimlessly. A rooster burst into life occasionally, irregularly, as if its watch had stopped and it was guessing at the time, hourly, until the sunrise. Owls hooted and passed their calls back and forth to each other. Cicadas chirped.

The golden circlet of tiny lights on the hills stayed on throughout the night. They were public streetlights, but with the kindness of distance turned into delicate jewels on the surrounding horizon.

It was hot, arid, very still. The marble floors came into their own, cooling and caressing your bare feet. The slightest movement in the lane made a noise.

Glyn was asleep upstairs in the guest room. Tim and Tom were on mattresses in what was to be our room. We were in the big brass bed we had bought with the house, which was on the ground floor at the back. Our bathroom was in the low-ceilinged w.c. adjacent to our room. I worried about using it in the dark, with no lights, but I discovered that the amber glow of the streetlights bathed the house in a pale light – not unattractive – which made padding about the house in the middle of the night quite safe.

I was too excited, and yet too tired, to sleep. I didn't think I would ever sleep again. We were in Italy now. We did it. We had moved our lives, and our hearts, to Italy. I didn't give too much thought to Wiltshire, or England, or Wales. The air here in Lazio was so thick and busy, it kept my mind entertained and engaged completely.

And then there were the boxes. Millions of boxes. We couldn't move for boxes, and this was just the first load. I couldn't face an Italian recycling centre; I hoped they would take all of our packing boxes kerbside. But who to ask? And did they speak English? And food? Was there a supermarket? When was our bank account going to open? Where was the bank? And the doctor? And the nearest hospital, if someone put their back out moving boxes? Surely someone in the village must speak English? I could always ring Andreas, I suppose, if I needed translating, but he had a hotel to run, wouldn't appreciate my continuing calls for translation. I finally sank into a fitful sleep, punctuated by the crowing of the rooster, half-dreaming, half-waking throughout the night.

A loud blast of Italian pop music, shot out from under the bed. It was morning. Somebody downstairs below us was awake. An Italian DJ rabbited on in a hyper, too-bright morning voice, annoying people into wakefulness. The daylight through the cracks in the shutters was blinding. I waited for the volume of the music to be adjusted, but somebody downstairs liked it loud. Our house had been vacant for some time, many years I thought, and all of our new neighbours had gotten used to living next to an uninhabited house. They had gotten out of the habit of consideration for others.

Suddenly, the church bells began to ring. It was 7.00. Clearly, the person downstairs had a clock radio set for 6.56, to allow themselves to wake up to the sound of pop music, before the sonorous sound of the church bells woke everyone else up at 7.00. The whole village must be hearing those bells, and that was the point: the church was the mainstay of the village and the church dictated when you woke up. Outside, somebody sped past in a car which needed a tune-up. How could anyone drive that fast in such a narrow lane? I heard the car noise disappear into the distance; it was amazing how long I continued to hear that car, even when it was a long way off.

Sandy needed to do her morning business. I had two choices: either take her out into the lane and hope she wouldn't be too fussy or take her up onto our little terracotta terrace. I couldn't face the world yet and wasn't in the mood to leap out of the way of a speeding car, so I tiptoed up the grand staircase, carrying my ancient dog, and encouraged her to do her business on the terrace. Even at 7.00 the tiles were heating up. They probably hadn't cooled down from the previous day. I wondered how hot it was going to be at noon.

No sign of Tim and Tom; no sign of Glyn. I thought *good, let them sleep, let me wake up slowly and gently*. Well, actually, too late for that.

Dear old Sandy. Lovely old dog. I wondered what she thought. No more soft Wiltshire grass, no more English garden birdsong. Well, she couldn't miss the birdsong, she'd been deaf and blind for years, but where she was once padding around a carpeted home and a garden laid to lawn, she was now picking her way up a long staircase, down cobbled streets, over cool marble floors.

She was settled back onto her little bed and I went to the kitchen, dodging the army of boxes blocking my way. We were using bottled water until the water had been tested, so I took a new bottle of mineral water, poured it into a saucepan (kettle was packed), and prepared to make coffee. The hob was a tiny, mean-spirited little gas thing, very incongruous in a country so in love with the culinary arts.

Luckily I had remembered to turn the refrigerator on, so the milk was fresh. The water boiled in the saucepan, and I poured it into the cafetiere, gave it a little stir and went to the sink to rinse my hands. I turned the tap. Nothing happened. Damn, air lock, I thought. How am I going to sort that? I don't know where anything is, in this big house, and I hadn't been paying attention when I was shown the clean and acrid boiler room during our house-hunting visit.

Maybe the water hadn't been turned on yet? I was worried. I was certain that Viv had arranged for everything to be working by the time we arrived. The loos had flushed last night, the shower was lovely. Maybe just the kitchen sink was air locked.

I went into the low-ceilinged loo. Same problem. No water. At the risk of waking Peter I flushed it. No water. Damn. What was going on? What had occurred overnight to turn the water off? I heard the sound of an elderly vacuum cleaner begin to buzz above us. Somebody else was up, and cleaning house. I wondered if they had water? I didn't need this shit. I needed water, to get the breakfasts going for everyone, to do last night's washing up.

Peter, who had magically slept through the clock radio, was now awake to the sound of the toilet handle rattling, the ballcock bouncing up and down merrily in an empty cistern. He staggered, half asleep to the door.

"What are you doing?" he mumbled, rubbing his eyes.

"There's no water. *DAMN*, I don't know why, but there's no water."

"What?"

I was irritated, having to repeat myself.

"*There's no water*. Not here, not in the kitchen."

"Did you try the bathroom upstairs?"

I had already been upstairs once, carrying Sandy to the terrace and back. I was getting grouchy.

"No, I have not tried the bathroom upstairs, I've just woken up. Correction: *I have just been woken up*. Did you hear that clock radio below us?"

"What?" Peter stifled a yawn.

I was about to get really tetchy, so I slipped past him and marched up the marble staircase for the second time towards the bathroom. On the second ascent I decided that I probably should wear slippers around the house, as the solid floors were beginning to make my bare feet ache. I quietly crept into the bathroom. Everyone else was still asleep. I tried the taps. No water. *Damn damn damn!* I stared out the bathroom window, listening to the methodical vacuuming above me, even louder on this floor. The view out of the window was mesmerising, and momentarily it distracted me from my anger. It was like a postcard, a florid and bountiful holiday snap. But of course, if I were on holiday, then no water would be somebody else's problem. But I wasn't on holiday. I was here. In our new house. With no water.

I decided that if I was going to be miserable, I was going to make other people miserable too. Misery loves company. I rang Viv, sod the early hour.

The phone rang in its odd, foreign-sounding ring.

Brrr. Brrr. Brrr. Brrr – *"Pronto?"*

She had at least answered but she was not happy about it.

"Viv? Hi, *we don't have any water.*" I couldn't be bothered with any of that *buongiorno* crap.

"Marcie?" She sounded sleepy.

"We don't have any water. I tried all of the taps. And there's a clock radio below us. And a manic vacuuming person above us. Did you turn the water on?"

"What?" She mumbled.

If I heard one more person say "What?" I was going to scream.

Now I felt like being really rude. She sold us a house with no water.

"There's no water in the fucking house!!!!"

There was a silence.

"Please don't swear at me."

I looked around for something to throw but the only option was a small travel toothbrush. Everything else was still packed.

"There's no water," I said, willing myself to calm down.

"That's because during summertime the council turns off the water each day for a period of time to conserve water. Most people have their own separate water tanks to cover for the period when the mains water is down."

"*What?*" I hissed. "Why didn't you tell us this when we bought the house?"

"Well," she said, speaking slowly and sarcastically, "because this happens all over Italy. It's even worse in the South. If you don't have a second backup tank then you're going to have to install one. We can arrange that for you."

I wondered if it was possible to throw the tiny travel toothbrush out of the window and up towards the incessant vacuuming.

"So what are we gonna do for today? When does it come back on? This is fucking ridiculous."

"Please don't swear at me."

"Damn it! Sorry. Gosh darn it."

I heard a noise behind me. I turned and looked out of the bathroom. Tim and Tom were standing, sleepy, waiting to use the loo.

"There's no water" I stated, trying to calm myself.

"Yes, we guessed that".

I think possibly I hadn't been as quiet as I should have been.

"Sorry. I'm sorry; I woke you up. I'm really sorry, I'm just a little upset."

They stared at me balefully.

"Sorry, come on in, go ahead, use the toilet, please, just don't flush. Use the one downstairs if you want to."

Tim shuffled past me and Tom headed for the stairs.

"There's coffee in the kitchen when you're ready" I said, artificially brightly, trying to make everything okay with just the tone of my voice.

I noticed on my way down the stairs, heat waves beginning to waver outside on the terrace. It was going to be a scorcher today, no doubt. I thought about Glyn, retraced my steps back up the stairs for the third time and peeked into his room. He was still sleeping soundly, legs half covered by the sheet he had kicked off in the night.

I padded down the steps again, heard a thud and a muffled curse. Tom had discovered the low ceilinged w.c. Even if you know it's low when you go in, it isn't easy to judge just how low it actually is until you make contact with the ceiling above.

I heard the rattle of the ballcock in the empty cistern. He'd already forgotten about the lack of water.

"There's no water, I'm afraid. Sorry." I tried to say this as kindly as possible through the closed door of the loo. "However, there is coffee, and it's really rather nice. *Lavazzo*. In the kitchen, when you're ready."

I padded out to the kitchen. My feet really *were* beginning to ache on those marble floors. I walked gingerly back to the ground floor bedroom to find my slippers in my suitcase, noting that the pop music had been turned off, and the hoovering had finished. Clearly it was possible to get back to sleep after 7.30 when everyone had gone off to work.

Peter had gone back to bed and was fiddling with his tablet trying to get a Wi-Fi signal. Italy has its own nationwide free Italian Internet, which I think is pretty impressive for a country to support its citizens like that. Peter was also getting some sort of WiFi signal from next door but he couldn't log in because he didn't know their password.

"Coffee?" I suggested, sliding on my slippers.

"Mmm, yes please."

"I'll bring it into you."

"Oh thanks, that's really kind, thank you."

I half walked, half ran all the way back to the kitchen, remembering Tom, and becoming conscious that this was a really large house. He was sitting at the dining table, with a cup of coffee in front of him, looking exactly as he had looked the night before. Clearly a night on a mattress on the marble floor had done him no favours. I decided not to ask him how he'd slept.

"I've got a sort of continental breakfast thing, if that's okay" I said overly jovially. "There's melon, and croissants, and bread, butter and fig jam, but I haven't found the toaster yet. Oh, and there's juice."

I had only brought three plates and mugs with me in the car, three sets of cutlery, and they were all dirty from last night. No water. I was going to have to heat bottled mineral water in the saucepan and do the washing up. Before breakfast. I didn't have a chef's knife to cut the melon. I was afraid to try the gas oven in case I had a problem, or it blew up or something. Anything was possible in this house. I put the croissants on the table, tidy in their little individually portioned plastic wrappers, with no apology for not heating them.

As I put the water on to boil, I could feel tension from across the room.

"We're really going to have to get going early, get a head start back to the U.K."

"Um, oh, okay. Sure. Let me just wash up these plates for breakfast and we'll get you on your way." The water was taking ages to boil.

"We don't have any money." He sounded like a broken record. "We're going to need cash for tolls and petrol. And food. We'll sleep in the cab again to save money and time."

"Right, okay, right, I'll just pop down to Peter and tell him you're asking."

The bedroom was actually further away from the kitchen then I had remembered. Now that I was criss-crossing back and forth down the length of the house I began to realise just how big it really was. The slippers helped, but I could still feel the impact of the marble on my feet through the soles of the slippers. Peter, having found the Italian Wi-Fi signal, was trawling through his emails, happily tucked up in the big brass bed. He had opened the shutters and the glory of Italy poured into the bedroom. There was a pretty little hilltop village across the valley, houses blending into the hillside, as they were all constructed from the local stone. This was the little golden tiara I had seen last night in the dark.

Gesturing at nothing in particular, Peter was beaming. "Look at that", he said proudly, as if he had built the entire village himself in my absence.

What a difference the sun makes! The evening before we had opened those same doors to admire the view across to the distant, jagged purple mountains. The most enormous hornet, the size of my *entire* thumb, had streaked angrily across the top of the frame and disappeared into the exterior eaves. Several more had followed suit, furious as hell. It was too hot to close the glass doors and there was a hair's breadth of netting between us an excruciating pain. To add to the misery, the heavy shutters which were designed to have metal clasps to hold them open had rusted and bent into useless coils of metal, hanging morosely against the outside wall. Later, once we'd settled in, if the afternoon sunlight was hot and strong I'd find myself forced to peel back the netting and reach out to shut the vented louvres, risking a painful sting from the hornets. I assigned this task forever, to my braver and calmer husband.

"Um, Tom wants to head off early, and he needs some money." It suddenly occurred to me that any sensible person would probably just nip down to the Ville del Colle, check into a nice room, have a good sleep and a shower, and spend the rest of the day relaxing in the pool. With a beer or two.

I, however, had a date with over a hundred large packing boxes, and I couldn't really decide where to start.

Things at last began to sort themselves out. The bottled mineral water boiled, the dishes were washed, the household was fed. Peter found a cash point and took out some money on his English account. Tim and Tom made a hasty exit, after a second cup of coffee and a stern talking to by Peter about finance. I don't think they had been extravagant with money during their journey down; I think that perhaps, like me, maths was a challenge for them and it was just difficult to keep track of costs during the trip. The primary reason why we had offered Tim this job was that he had moved his parents to Spain, and this seemed to qualify as experience in our minds. Having just come across from Wiltshire in or own 4x4 made me realise just how big France was, and just how far away we really were.

English people who travel in the States often remark that they have seriously misjudged the distances on maps. In the U.K. you can plan a route from, say, Cumbria to Manchester and it really isn't that far on a map. But when you decide to travel across the U.S. from, let's say, Colorado to Pennsylvania, it is really, really far, and it's so easy to get caught out by getting the sheer scale of the country wrong.

I had looked at the big atlas in Wiltshire and seen virtually a straight diagonal line from southern England to Rome. You just hop across the English Tunnel, biff through France, and suddenly, bingo, you're at the French/ Italian border before you know it, and you're nearly in Rome. Well, that's how it looks when you're sitting at the dining table with a glass of wine, a pencil and a ruler.

But for Tom and Tim, sitting in the cab of a van in the heat with no cigarette lighter, money, or phone signal, it was a very long journey. I hadn't asked him anything about his parents' move to Spain, but I now realised it was probably shorter, cooler, and buffered by the support of his grateful parents. And it didn't involve paying tolls on the autostrada, or going through southern Germany.

The two men bundled up their things, grabbed some croissant packets and Nutella for the journey, and climbed into the van. Peter confirmed their route and off they went with a perfunctory wave. As they drove off, they took their gloom with them. I returned to the house, feeling lighter and more cheerful. We still had no water, but we were now able to begin savouring our ownership.

I looked up and down the pretty little cobbled lane: this was *our lane* now. I slid my hand reverently across the big wooden door as I entered: this was *our door* now. I loved the way your eyeline naturally rose up to the graceful, vaulted ceiling in the entry hall, and then floated through a pair of ancient half-glazed, family-crested interior doors and up the splendid staircase.

Back in the kitchen I rummaged through some of the kitchen cupboards and found a chef's pan, an elderly grill pan, some even more elderly cooking oil, and what I soon discovered to be a chestnut roaster. That really captured my imagination: imagine roasting chestnuts in the autumn! I also found several packets of plastic plates and cutlery, and paper cups. This was a sign to me that perhaps this was not the first time the house had been without water, and that washing up was not always an option.

I heard a noise upstairs; Glyn was awake and rattling the handle of the toilet upstairs.

"Mum?" he called down the stairs, "There's something wrong with the toilet."

"Yes sweetheart, I know. Good morning! Welcome to Italy! We'll sort it. It'll all get sorted. Would you like me to bring you some breakfast?"

"Yeah, sure, thanks, that'd be great."

I heard him pad back to his room, and I grabbed a handful of breakfast things for him. As I climbed the stairs for the fourth time that morning, I was beginning to feel it in my thighs a bit. And my feet. Puffing slightly, I laid everything out on a little table for him, opened the two pairs of shutters and the French doors out onto the terrace, filling the room with blinding light, warmth and the sounds of the street. He squinted against the sunlight, curled back up on his bed. I adjusted the shutters a bit and closed the glass windows against the noise.

"Viv said something about conserving water, I'm not quite sure what that's all about. Anyway, don't worry about it. Daddy'll sort it. If need be, we might be able to go back to the hotel for a shower." I thought wistfully of the cool embrace of the swimming pool, the *risotto con funghi*, the hot shower with great water pressure. All of it just a mere three minutes' drive down the lane.

"Right, sweetheart, now that you're sorted for breakfast, take it easy this morning, you've had a long night. Make sure you've packed all your things by noon so we can catch your flight. I'm going to make a start on these boxes."

We were due to take him to Rome later that day, to catch a flight back to Cardiff, via Dublin. I tried to ignore the painful stab in my heart; he was leaving.

I shuffled down the stairs again for the fourth time, now using the elaborately wrought iron handrail for support. I decided that the most urgent boxes would be in the kitchen. I could hear Peter humming under his breath in the guest bedroom which was always a good sign. As long as he wore his slippers and kept his head tucked down low in the w.c. he should be fine.

The first kitchen box yielded champagne flutes and a port decanter with no lid. Very useful. Herbs and spices and a slightly leaky plastic bottle of safflower oil came next, followed by a large platter with a Christmas motif on it, and a pair of napkin ring holders from our wedding.

Where was the useful stuff? I wondered. In the house purchase we had also bought a cavernous half glazed cupboard, rather cheaply and poorly constructed, but good for storage. I was so glad we did. This cupboard, magically, never seemed to fill up no matter how much you put in it, so everything I unpacked that was irrelevant went in there. I had no idea what was in these boxes as I hadn't been there when the packers did their pack, so it was potluck really, opening each box, hoping for something helpful like the toaster, cutlery, or the microwave. I came across a box filled with bedding and towels, but I couldn't face another trip up the stairs that morning, so I dragged it through the hallway to the base of the stairs and decided it was going to be someone else's problem.

I continued to re-discover my joy of the place, my pride in our choice of house, and country. I heard sounds from the street filtering through the windows, and they were exciting sounds, new, foreign. Dogs barked, women greeted each other and gossiped in Italian, church bells rang, shoes clipped across the cobblestones. Somewhere a radio was turned on.

We had a break at lunchtime and took Glyn off to the airport, a ninety-minute trip each way. I tried to breathe deeply and not panic. This was always going to be the plan, but now that we were actually at this point I couldn't bear the thought of him leaving. It was too far. I tried to picture him with his new uni friends, having drinks at *Wetherspoons*, larking about, and laughing together.

It was all going to be okay.

Settling in

"We have dived, headlong, into The Italian Way. We are not in Tourist Italy now, we are in the Italy that remains when other people's vacations are over, when the holiday makers have gone home at the end of the summer."

In the week that ensued, we swung, pendulum-like, between extreme comfort and extreme discomfort. The comfort was usually connected in some way, to food or scenery. The extreme discomfort usually related to weather and personal hygiene.

A perfect mid-morning espresso, poured carefully into my favourite demi-tasse cups, enjoyed under the big umbrella on the terrace, and accompanied by more of Antoinette's pink wafer biscuits, was heaven. Shopping in the tiny village store, carefully unwrapping my culinary treasures and preparing a simple lunch, was really what it was all about.

The lack of water never seemed to be at the same time. Sometimes it went off in the evening, sometimes in the morning. Between 4.00p.m. and 7.00a.m. was a nightmare. I've heard it said that it takes six weeks to form a new habit; I never got used to this. It was frankly disgusting. Even after we did sort the problem, I would turn the taps on hesitantly, praying for the simple joy of water in the taps.

I had come to Italy to write, and the words poured out of me. I was keeping a journal, hosting a blog site, photographing everything that caught my eye and posting on social media, writing to my friends. We were in the first blush of our honeymoon, in which everything which was good was going to be good for ever, and everything that went wrong was just a temporary little hiccup.

I wasn't particularly homesick for Britain, but I did miss my boys. The boxes kept me busy, and the newness of our different lives distracted me from being maudlin. But the maternal ache of absent children was like a dull throb in my heart daily. We were the ones who had left. We were the ones who were trying to re-invent ourselves after two decades of successful parenting. The boys seemed to be doing fine without us. My early journal entries were blinded by love for the house: *"I feel as though I am being let into a special secret: Italy in the Off-Season. I am living here now, full-time, suitcases tucked away neatly on top of the wardrobe, and am about to experience the Italy that travel agents warn you against when booking your holidays. November Italy. It's thrilling and scary at the same time. We don't know enough about the house to know how it will weather a winter, and I just sort of keep my head down and picture this house, having survived all of its four centuries intact, with grace and elegance..."*

JOURNAL ENTRIES

OLIVE-PICKING

Many people around the valley had begun picking their olives this week, and everywhere you went you could see various types of olive-harvesting devices. The smoke from olive-wood bonfires daily fills the air. The people below us had a rickety petrol-driven sort of paddle on an extended pole; the paddle seemed to gently shake the treetops and shake the olives down without damaging the branches or the fruit. Other people were picking by hand.

Everywhere there were huge nets to gather the olives, and the women seemed to be given the task of hauling the huge, filled nets up to the waiting trucks. Most women seemed beautifully dressed for the occasion; one lady I waved to was elegantly dressed in a smart black jersey knit top and gold jewellery. I don't really see a lot of sportswear around here, and certainly not a lot of work clothes. I have seen several pinnies, though, so I guess wearing a protective pinnie allows you to wear your nice clothes and still get something useful done around the house.

CHURCH BELLS

The house itself is solid, stentorian, timeless. Next to it, the church, is a small and intricate confection of a church, which used to be the private church for the family who inhabited the palazzo. It is intimate and grand at the same time, and is now used for village services. Inside there is a statue of Madonna and Child, with the most exquisite faces. It was made with great care, and great love. The sound of singing floating out of the door on hot summer evenings is indescribably beautiful.

Daily, a pair of jovial bell ringers troop up the hill for the late afternoon session. One of them is our lovely cleaning lady, Teresa. She is only available to clean until 11.55a.m., as she needs to belt off and ring the noontime bell. When we first met her she tried to mime this information to us, having not a word of English, and she repeated the word campanello. I sat there stoically typing the word into my Google translate app, and after the translation finally came up: bell, I looked at my watch and realized that she had only two minutes to dash up to the church for the lunchtime bell. I have no idea how she managed it but dead on twelve noon the bells chimed. The bell ringers, when they appear, are fun and good-humoured, and a sign that the day is beginning to wind down. Often, the grace of the bells compete with the static and grainy sounding pop radio station from next door, but somehow they complement each other perfectly.

SHOPPING

One of my greatest delights is to pad down the small, serious lane, to the local shop. I prefer the cool of the morning. Beautiful designs have been embedded into the cobblestones of the piazza, in multi- coloured patterns of granite and marble. A simple design in front of the church commemorates the building of the church: Chiesi 1602. A gentle statue of San Lorenzo blesses the square, arm held high holding a delicate crucifix. Pots, bottles, and a rather incongruous metal Ballantyne's scotch presentation box hold floral offerings and are placed with love around the base of the statue. Small, red, battery-operated votive candles are popular in Italy, and you see their small illuminations in the evenings, flickering gently at the foot of the statue of each town's local saint, or namesake. Two marble cobblestone stripes lead the way down the lane, past large and small houses — some crumbling ancient properties, some post-war new builds, but each with their own personality and charm.

I went into the shop last night for baking powder. I'm not good at baking, so most of the baking related products in my larder go out of date because I don't bake very often. Six-year-old baking powder went in the circular file, and off we went to the shops.

Well actually, initially we went to the shop for oranges. La Bottega, as it was called, was the only shop in Colli, but somehow managed to have nearly everything you wanted, despite its modest size. Four shelves alone were dedicated exclusively to dried pasta, in a myriad of shapes and sizes.

Sophia and her husband owned it, and ran it together in shifts. Sophia was the essence of generosity. It's a miracle that they ever made a profit. Rarely did I leave there without an armful of fresh herbs, maybe some lovely flowers from her garden, once a slice of cactus which she taught me how to cut carefully to eat. They know me well in that shop and are very good at tempting me with little hints like "Tomorrow is the day for fruit and vegetable delivery. Would you like some?" How can I resist? I just popped in for a moment, so I didn't have a shopping list translated into Italian, and I didn't have my phone with Google Translate on it. I fully expected to see, next to the bags of flour, neat little tubs of Baking Powder and Baking Soda., like they have in Britain. No such luck. Below the flour were tinned tomatoes, and next to the flour was semolina, and nowhere in the shop could I find anything remotely looking like baking powder.

Now, some items are easy to mime and some are not, and some are just embarrassing to mime (like 'jellyfish'). Baking powder is one of them. I mimed stirring a mixture in a bowl, I pointed to the biscuits, I mimed billowing clouds of food product meant to resemble a raising agent like baking powder. The very kind and very patient gentleman behind the till went straight to the refrigerator and brought out fresh yeast. I waved "no" in a Charades-like gesture and looked for a packet of biscuits. Scanning down the list of ingredients I found what I suspected to be the raising agents and I pointed this out to him. He looked baffled, and then handed me a slim envelope with a Victorian-style images of angels on it, holding a beautifully baked vanilla sponge cake. I thought perhaps it might be anjelica. He then showed me the same sort of packet, but with pictures of bread and pizza on it. Whatever it was, there was a sweet and savoury version of it, so it couldn't possibly be baking powder. I thought he was giving me dried yeast so again I said no.

People began piling into the shop, looking vaguely annoyed at having been stuck behind The American in the queue, taking up time and not knowing the Italian for anything. One or two ladies were quite helpful, as they observed my mime skills and discussed what the mysterious ingredient might be.

I decided that, if I did in fact buy dried yeast, the pudding I was hoping to make would be bit cake-like rather than pudding-like and that this wouldn't be a major crime and I really did need to relinquish my place in the queue. so that the other good people in the shop could get home to their loved ones. So I bought the angel-emblazoned packet of mystery ingredient.

Once home I Googled and discovered the most delightful product. Vanilla flavoured baking powder. With angels on it. How gorgeous. The vanilla-flavoured baking powder made angelic sweet cakes and biscuits, and the savoury baking powder made angelic breads and dough. I stared at the image of the angels. They looked so proud of their heavenly products, and the packet looked so pretty sitting on the shelf of my larder. I was so proud of this new purchase: so Italian, and so sensible, and ever-so-slightly eccentric, and so dainty sitting next to the great dusty sacks of flour and dried pasta in my larder. I wanted to share this moment with someone, but I didn't think that anyone else would be terribly interested. I settled for a private moment of reflection and introspection.

At Isola de Liri Market Day this morning we recognized some market stalls from other villages. I guess they make the rounds to each village throughout the week. I suppose we will begin to recognize our favourite stalls and will be able to anticipate what to buy each week. I still can't summon up the courage to haggle. If I ask the price of something, and I think it is too high, I can only just muster a look of annoyance as I walk away. No one ever calls me back with a counteroffer.

We found a new deli stall today, and a delightful stall owner who really made an effort. His huge wheels of cheese were dappled with coloured rind, and he proudly explained that the salamis were from his own pig. He was quite insistent that we try his cheeses and he slivered into a large semi-hard wheel for us to taste. It was very punchy, salty, and delicious.

"Pecorino Romano?" I asked. He puffed up and looked

offended.

"Pecorino *MIO!*" He declared.

He had travelled across from the Abruzzo region with his goods, which must have been a bit hair-raising as that would have taken him across the Apennines at some point. After the big storm the first snowfall of the season could be seen on the distant mountains, and I'm not sure by which route he had made it to us this morning, but we enjoyed it all the more, knowing it had come so far. A salty, aged Pecorino with ripe honeydew melon is indescribably wonderful.

I've been moaning about the lack of fish. I'm not really a fishy person, and tend to stick to my one or two safe favourites, but unfortunately salmon, smoked salmon, and shelled prawns are very British, and I must cultivate some new favourites over here. I wrote down and translated a list of my favourite seafoods into Italian, but haven't seen many of them over here; there is an entire ocean of unfamiliar Italian fish that I must now reckon with. The curiously-named John Dory mystifies me: it sounds so English!

I went in a proper fish shop today: Il Mediterraneo, just around the corner from the Isola de Liri market. I was quite stunned when I went in. The fish smell was very fresh, and very overpowering. There were vast tanks with things swimming, and huge glistening piles of fish of all sorts, some whole, and large mounds of filleted and gutted fish as well. A huge grey chopping block stood in the centre of the shop, with a waiting cleaver. There at the back was a beautifully displayed half side of salmon, which I'd been scouting for all week. I lost my nerve and asked for only half of the half side, which somewhat spoiled the display afterwards, but now that I know where to find great fish I'll make the grand gesture and take the whole piece. My husband was hovering over our dubiously parked car, so I had braved the fish shop on my own. I wasn't really clear whether or not I was meant to haggle over the fish, so I shyly paid the asking price, hoping I wasn't looking too foreign, or too foolish.

LAUNDRY

The Art of Laundry is a big issue out here. There must be a million and one ways to dry a sheet. Clotheslines are slung rakishly across the rooftops of the valley; on sunny days washing of all sorts punctuates the verdant valley floor. I have seen colourful swags of washing lines, peppered with clothes pegs, and simple blankets draped across railings. I've seen elaborate pulley systems run precariously across village lanes, sheets drying on bushes, and simple rows of children's clothes, waving like party bunting from city apartment windows. My favourite invention was a small Juliet balcony in Naples, with a graceful, armless, dressmaker's mannequin, sporting wet clothes drying in the summer sun. My washing hangs on ornate iron railings across my French windows.

I was very tentative at first bout hanging our own wet laundry to dry out of doors in the baking, dry heat. It was the stuff of movies, or postcards from European destinations. It isn't very Californian, or at least not part of the 1960s suburban Orange County I grew up in. We all had our tumble dryers, our dishwashers, and our jumbo clothes-washers. Relying on Nature to do something for us was just not really an option. Out onto the little terracotta terrace I went with my little clothes horse and a handful of wet clothes. Saturated, actually. An elderly clothes washer had been included in the house purchase, but the labels were all in Italian, the instruction manual long gone. I couldn't decipher where 'spin-dry' was on the dial. Everything that went into that machine came out sopping. I only hung out exterior clothing. I worried that a gust of wind might blow my bras and pants onto the neighbouring terraces. The soggy clothes hung grimly to the rails until they appeared bolstered by the arm breeze. It was as if their spirits had lifted. The clothes actually began to look lighter. The warm air swept all around the terrace, polishing the terracotta tiles, brushing-up the apricot colour plaster walls. The clothes were tinder dry in no time at all. It sounds so naff to be waxing lyrical about laundry but, after a machine-operated suburban childhood, this was pretty cool.

NIGHTS

Nights are magical. My new neighbourhood is steep and ragged, with chasm river valleys and razor-edged peaks. The Italian love of building on mountain tops is very much in evidence here. These aren't exceptionally high peaks, but they are gaspingly steep, veined with small switchback hairpin roads that cut back and forth up the hillside, usually to a monastery, or nunnery. At night, these little hilltops are crowned with jewelled lights, tiny fairy light strings of streetlights that crown the hilltops like tiaras.

I was quick to tell our friends about the good things in our new life, but something held me back from revealing the problems. For the most part everyone seemed delighted for us that we had done the Awfully Big Adventure and if there were any green-eyed monsters lurking about I never saw them. We had already made arrangements for three of our friends to visit, and the boys at Christmastime.

But the water problem was emotionally draining. The simplest house chores became complicated. Viv sent a pair of slightly shifty-looking plumbers to inspect and measure up for installing a second tank. They conversed stealthily in Italian to each other, peered up at the existing high-level cistern, made notes, asked her to translate. The quote went up and up, as they included plumbing parts, labour, timber to make a framework for the tank, a new tank, re-plastering, and re-decorating.

No one had yet answered our simple question: how did Lucio and Antoinette manage living in the house before us? They looked to me like the sort of erudite, cosmopolitans who wouldn't have stood for any substandard living arrangements. News began to trickle in about them: this was their summer place. Or perhaps, more likely, their spring and autumn place. Summer would've been off limits due to the lack of air conditioning – and water. The charm and simplicity of rural life could be enjoyed for perhaps a week or two, or possibly only a weekend. But they were Roman residents now; no doubt any home improvements had been spent on their city home, not this one.

One balmy evening, we met the neighbours, and learned more.

I was, and still am, extremely shy, and would often spend two, three days on end never setting foot outside for fear of meeting people. Even poor old Sandy was adverse to life outside of our ancient stone walls. Being blind made her wary of walking down hills and slopes, and I think the cobblestones were painful on her elderly paws. She was uncomfortable too, in the heat, and spent entire afternoons barely moving, on the cool spot where Antoinette's large cushion had been, at the meeting of two breezes from two pairs of French doors. At her age, all she could really manage happily was a few trips a day up and down the staircase, and visits to the terrace when nature called. A slightly sloping floor and a clever set of drains ensured that the terrace was able to be kept clean and tidy with regular swabbings of hot soapy water.

But on this particular evening as I prepared to walk up to the car for some reason or another, suddenly the neighbourhood came to life. We had noticed that the man across the lane had a small table and two small chairs perched just outside his front door, safe from passing cars. He was in the habit of sitting outside of an evening, with a beer or two and, like moths to the flame, the village would arrive. Never more than two or so, at a time, and often different people, but frequently there were men in the lane, laughing, gossiping, tossing football results around, punctuating the hot, still air with shouts of approval or disapproval.

Mercifully, he was The Man in The Village Who Spoke English. As we opened our giant studded front door, he suddenly appeared in his doorway, wielding a handful of beers.

"Hello!" he called, grinning broadly, waving the bottles aloft. "How are you? Welcome to Colli! Would you like a drink?"

He was slim and compact, dark but not Italian-looking. His English was heavily accented.

He gestured to his little table with the bottles. "Welcome to the Green Bar!"

I think it was a reference to the tidy piece of Astroturf laid out beneath the table. I just smiled and nodded. Peter smiled back and crossed the three steps it took to leave our house and join him at his table. We were so relieved to hear English spoken at last.

"I am Jaka," he said, opening two of the bottles, "I am from Slovenia."

At my side suddenly appeared a small, wide, and friendly woman, dark-haired, with the saddest eyes I'd ever seen.

"*Buonasera*," she said.

"*Buonasera*," I replied, using up nearly all of my Italian vocabulary with that one word.

She put a hand to her chest. "Lucia," she said, "*mi chiamo Lucia.*"

I was fascinated to see someone smile with sad eyes. It confused me. I also put my hand to my chest. "I'm Marcie." I felt Sandy brush next to my leg. "This is my dog Sandy."

"*Buonasera cagnolino*," she said, reaching down calmly to pat her.

I continued to speak in English, with accompanying mime.

"She's old, and deaf, and blind."

"Ooh," Lucia said, squatting down to caress her ears. "*Bellissimo.*"

The men had clinked bottles and were settling comfortably into the makeshift bar.

Lucia gestured for me to follow her and signalled for Sandy to follow as well.

We went inside her tiny house, two doors away. It looked to be one room on the ground floor and possibly one upstairs, as I thought I glimpsed a staircase in the rear of the room. Perhaps the second room was downstairs; I really couldn't tell. It was painted a vibrant orange. There was a small table, a tiny cooker, and what looked to be a shrine surrounding the photo of a good-looking young man. This explained the sad eyes.

Lucia saw my gaze and gestured to her heart. Her smile now matched her eyes: a tragic smile. I realised in an instant that this was what her life was all about: the memory of this boy. He could have been her son, perhaps her grandson. He was gone, he was mourned, he was remembered.

I noticed something bubbling away in oil on the stove; it looked to be *stracciatella*, the leftover strands of mozzarella production. I had seen it made once on a tour of a mozzarella dairy, and it was most commonly used to fill the inside of a ball of *burrata*.

As I turned away from the stove, I was too late to prevent Lucia offering Sandy a tidbit of food, I wasn't sure what exactly. Sandy sniffed it and wolfed it whole, promptly vomiting all over Lucia's floor. I was mortified, racking my brains how to explain with mime.

"Ahh, No, um, no food *solida*!" I said, panicking, miming like mad, making up Italian vocabulary as best I could. "*Diolch yn fawr iawn*," I continued, slipping accidentally into Welsh. Welsh was never there when I needed it, in Wales, but cropped up unexpectedly in foreign countries, (and also, occasionally, a bit of French which I studied for one year only in junior high school). No helpful and appropriate Italian words entered my anxious mind at this moment; it was Welsh, English, or nothing.

She gestured nonchalantly and picked up a dustpan and brush, scraping the gelatinous vomit into the pan and wandering off into the back, presumably to the w.c. I stood there, mortified. What a way to meet the neighbourhood. This would be all over the village by morning, I had a feeling.

She ambled back in, still the sad eyes but the smile was back, the saddest smile. "*Mea culpa*," I stammered, although it wasn't strictly true. It was a botched veterinary procedure which nearly killed my poor dog, and she had been on borrowed time, fragile and ancient, ever since.

Lucia waved away the entire incident with a single gesture and invited me to sit at her table. The stracciatella bubbled merrily away – I'd never seen it cooked before – and I sat gingerly on my chair, taking in this most foreign and unusual little sitting room, stroking my disappointed dog.

I wondered how the menfolk were getting on in the Green Bar. I wanted to connect with Lucia somehow, my heart was very full with feeling. I gazed at the shrine, little votive candles and the framed young man. I looked across at her, touched my hand to my heart and just met her eyes for a moment. It was all I could manage, but it was enough.

There was a small pause, and I felt I should go.

"*Mi scusi*," I said, gesturing vaguely towards our house. She nodded and smiled, giving Sandy one last stroke of the ears before we went back out into the balmy night, and towards the sounds of laughter.

The men were having a great time, collapsed back in the patio chairs, helpless with laughter. Beer bottles littered the table. They had been joined by another man, a dark-haired middle aged Italian man who I recognized as living immediately next door to us. The noise, amplified by the narrow lane, shot up and down the street.

"*He is! He is! Busta da balls guy!*" announced Jaka, prompting more laughter. I smiled, not having a clue what was being said. Lucia spoke to them in Italian and a rapid exchange ensued. I think she was telling them that my dog threw up in her kitchen, but maybe it was chat about the weather.

They all looked sympathetically at me except Peter who didn't understand.

"Sandy threw up on her kitchen floor," I hissed at him, reliving the moment in my mind. Peter looked shocked. "She gave her something to eat; I don't know what. It's fine, it's okay, she cleaned it up." Peter looked even more horrified, but I waved away the incident with a simple gesture, as Lucia had done in the house. I was learning to use my hands now, speaking with them instead of words.

Jaka leaned forward in his chair, suddenly serious. He poked the beer bottle in the air, punctuating his sentences.

"No really, I mean, it: *there is something wrong with your house*. Lucio he is not nice man. He ask me to come work for him and I didn't want to and I look around that house. There is much wrong with it. You will see."

I stared at him. Great. Ghosts. Earthquake damage. Dead bodies buried in the basement. I suddenly felt a bit sick.

"Okay, okay, enough already!" said Peter, still chuckling as he got up from his seat. "Thanks for the beer, Jaka. Nice to meet you Antonio." He offered his hand to our neighbour and they shook. We waved our goodbyes and went the three steps back across the lane into our cavernous front doorway, guiding Sandy gently over the threshold.

"*Buonanotte. Ciao ciao!*" We had learned from Viv to say ciao twice, which I took to mean "*bye bye*". No one ever seemed to leave without saying ciao several times to each other.

"*Ciao ciao!*" they chorused. I gave an extra little wave to Lucia who was heading back to her home, and she waved. "*Ciao!*"

"*Ciao ciao,*" and we were finally inside.

"What the hell was that all about?" I said, giggling and worried at the same time.

"Oh it's nothing, don't worry. I think our friend Jaka is a bit dramatic."

"Why? What's he said?"

"Well, you heard him; he thinks there's something wrong with the house."

"What, you mean apart from not having running water during daylight hours?" I said, irked.

"Well, no, you know that's to do with the council and water conservation."

"I'm sorry but, why on earth would the council turn off the water supply during the hours when everyone is awake and using it? Why not turn it off throughout the night when everyone is asleep?" I was feeling heated.

Peter waved away the comment and shrugged his shoulders. He too was learning body language.

"No, he was talking about something else. He's an electrician. It's something to do with the electrics."

Ahh. Now that explained a lot.

There was an ancient, grime encrusted toaster oven abandoned in the kitchen, but when I had tried to use it, it fused the lights. When I tried to use the electric cooker, the lights fused. I thought there might be a leak in the sink which meant water was cutting out the electrics, but this was a bit more sinister. It meant possibly the whole system was at fault.

"Oh. That's not good."

"No," Peter said, climbing the stairs heavily. "Please don't worry. I'm sure he's just having a bit of fun with us."

I scooped up Sandy in my arms and carried her up the stairs. She increasingly found them insurmountable. She was so frail it was hardly a burden.

Later that night, in bed, I thought back over everything that had happened. Lucia and the shrine, Lucio, Antoinette. I really must learn Italian, *presto*, otherwise life was going to be very hard, and very lonely.

The next morning after a cold breakfast, and hot cafetiere coffee made on the gas hob, Peter rang Viv.

"Viv, we're having some problems with the electrics. Can you please send someone around to have a look? We haven't had a bill yet, either. And how long will it be before the plumbers can add our extra tank?"

She sounded irritated. "I'll find out and get back to you."

Peter hung up, not happy.

"Well, I'm sure these are all just little teething troubles. Little hiccups. We'll get some more bottled water from the shop. Jaka suggested a supermarket which he calls *Spendi Bene*, just up the road. It's a discount supermarket. He topped up our coffee cups and put the cafetiere in the sink.

"Now I do have some good news, which I think you'll like. There's going to be a street party here next week, an annual wine festival." We'd seen evidence of these as we travelled around Lazio. Each town took turns having their own autumn celebration, sometimes sharing the same street decorations, and now it was our turn.

"You can make food and sell it at your own stall, if you want to. Jaka says everybody does; they're not professional chefs, they're just town residents, but he says the food is always amazing and it's good fun. They turn the whole village into the party, every street is used. There's music and lots of wine."

I thought briefly of what my stall might look like: California-style Cobb salad, Caesar salad, composed salads, vegetable salads. It sounded like fun but shyness began to creep up from the floor.

"I think maybe I'll just watch this time," I said

"Okay, suit yourself. We'll just go and do a reccy."

I went up to the bedroom to do some journal writing, settling into my favourite chair, looking out through the French windows onto the staggering vista across the valley, warm and pink in the morning sun. It was so beautiful here. How could anything possibly be wrong in such a gorgeous country?

There was still an army of boxes blocking my every move, but I was trying to pace myself, little and often, so I didn't get overwhelmed. *Just be patient*, I counselled myself. *It'll be fine. It'll all be okay.*

BLOG POST: COLLI WINE FESTIVAL

The Colli Wine Festival did in fact have wine as its theme, but the wine on offer was more along the lines of a thread linking a wide variety of stalls and events. For 5 Euros we were given a map and a small cotton pouch on a long strap, which neatly contained a plastic wine glass. This was our entry to the Wine Festival, and at any stall you cared to visit, a jug of wine would be on offer for free refills.

We were told that the food on offer was "street food", created by stall owners, exclusively for street festivals, and not available during the rest of the year in a shop or restaurant. This gave a special frisson to the occasion, a fresh, one-off carpe diem sort of event, virtually an entire "pop up" street village, created for one night only, each year.

Live bands played, lit by bright fete lighting, and the music rebounded off the villas and church walls.

Slim strings festooned the street above our heads, decorated with cartoons of wine glasses, fairies, wine lovers, and festive images.

Colli is primarily laid out in one long ancient lane, and the festival coiled its way up one side and down the next; it was impossible to see the end in either direction. Piped in recorded music blared from one end of the street, and then subtly morphed into the street bands, and tapered off into in the darkness down the other side. On an ordinary day the little village is quiet and sedate, punctuated with church bells at regular intervals, laughter and gossip from cheerful neighbours, passing the time of day in front of their houses. But it blossomed into a large exotic flower on this evening, and villagers packed the tiny lane shoulder-to-shoulder, well into the next morning.

The joy of "street food" is its simplicity, its portability, and its ability to stabilize you between glasses of wine. On offer were high-carb items such as pizza, fried pizza, and jacket potatoes filled with a variety of toppings such as lamb stew.

Freshly made potato chips were huge, incredibly crispy, and made right in front of you in boiling cauldrons, laid out next to vast piles of potatoes.

Hot braziers flared, and an enormous drum filled with hot coals and roasting chestnuts was manned by a kindly woman, cheeks flushed with the heat.

Deep fried scampi and calamari were cooked to order, freshly dredged in seasoned flour and served in paper cones with a wedge of lemon.

A large display of homemade cakes and pies was laid out immediately outside of my front doorstep, and strategically situated near the ticket booth.

There is a particular skill required at street festivals: balancing your glass, your food, and your conversation simultaneously. The cleverer partyers bought paper cones of street food and tucked them into their cloth pouches, leaving one hand free to hold the glass, and another hand free to gesticulate while chatting. I retired comparatively early, but I stole out onto our balcony to see how things were progressing, round about midnight, and I saw nothing but contented faces, happy families, young people laughing and smiling. No one was yelling, no one was throwing bottles, no one was getting sick or antagonizing people, it was just the kindest, friendliest gathering of a community that I had ever seen.

As I understand it, street, wine, and food festivals take place all over Italy, throughout the year, a steady stream of celebrations for the glorious cornucopia that is the Italian countryside. In Colli I saw people of all ages, babes in arms to grandparents, and great grandparents. This is how communities thrive and survive: an unspoken agreement to unite each year with the gifts of food and wine, to celebrate togetherness, and uniqueness, and all things joyfully, and ebulliently, Italian.

Peter had had further conversations with Jaka about the water situation in our house. He seemed surprisingly well informed about it. And the electrics. I wondered if perhaps the house had been the subject of much gossip in the village over the years.

Peter asked Jaka to come have a look downstairs in the boiler room, and he duly arrived one evening with a plumbing friend of his. I stayed in the kitchen, boiling up pots of bottled mineral water to do the washing up. They returned to the kitchen, looking grim.

"Do you want the good news or the bad news?" Peter asked, grabbing a handful of beers from the fridge.

"Um, good news first please."

"*We have a backup tank.* A huge backup water tank right there in a room next to the boiler room. Viv, Lucio and Antoinette never mentioned it."

"Oh that's great news! Fantastic! We just saved having to hire those guys to come put a tank in and tear up the walls. So what's the bad news?"

He flipped open the bottles and passed them around. "Our water supply is connected to the downstairs apartment."

"What? What do you mean?"

Suddenly it all came out. Lucio's family had all lived in this ancestral home, which had expanded greatly over the years. Over time various branches of the family had taken over separate wings of the palazzo, but nobody had ever bothered to separate out the utilities. It had all stayed in the family. Lucio was the first family member to break the family circle and sell off his part of the palazzo to outsiders.

When we had first spotted this house in the estate agent listings it was offered for sale either together with the coach house below or separately as two independent properties. We had chosen the top two floors, and the unconverted coach house below was still on the market. It was difficult to make out if the electrics were also joined together but the water certainly was.

There was plenty of evidence of the house having been connected to next door. The floor plans, dating from the 1930s, showed that some of the communal doorways had been sealed off and made into cupboards, some for our house and some for next door. In fact, on the ground floor there was still a bolted door into our neighbour's apartment which we couldn't open, but which nobody had bothered to plaster over.

I could imagine a situation in which a young couple marries and moves into a set of apartments. Nobody is going to make it awkward by asking them to put in their own utilities and pay independently for them. Families just don't work that way. We were still as connected to that noble family – and their services – just as if we were merely house guests staying over for, well, we thought for the rest of our lives.

"How much is *that* going to cost us?" I asked, passing round some crisps.

"Well, the water tank is sorted. It's on. Jaka just had to turn a tap and it began running in straight away."

"You mean we'll never have our water cut off again? That's fantastic!" I looked at the army of mineral water bottles on the floor and smiled.

"We're fine until someone buys the downstairs apartment. Then we have to deal with the situation. Or we just take over the water supply ourselves, and downstairs has to put in their own supply."

"And the electrics?" Jaka turned to his friend and chatted animatedly in Italian.

His friend shrugged and swigged his beer.

"He say maybe, who knows?" Jaka said. "You have to have someone look at the wiring. He think maybe you have power cut because you don't have enough power in your system – maybe your system, it is old – so when you run too many thing at the same time it is – how you say – overload."

I felt like I was on a rollercoaster. The delight at having non-stop water had faded in the light of news that we only had enough electricity to charge an electric toothbrush, and who knew what would happen when downstairs – in the future – tried to charge his electric toothbrush at the same time?

"And another thing..." Peter continued, fiddling with the crisp packet, "that funny smell you mentioned in the boiler room? That's diesel. Our central heating system runs on diesel oil."

"Is that bad?"

"Well, it's not cheap. It's just an old system, and needs to be updated."

I stared at the large chunky radiator in the dining room, picturing one in every room, counting up ten or more throughout the house.

"So: *that's* why this house was such a bargain."

"There's no such thing as a bargain in property sales, I'm afraid," said Peter. "If a house is going cheap, there's probably a reason."

"Great."

Is that why we weren't getting any electricity bills? Or water bills? How much of this did Viv know about? I was beginning to get very suspicious, and very depressed, in equal measure. We had yet to meet our hoover-mad neighbour next door. All we knew was that she was a relative of Lucio, a sister I think; a retired teacher, with no English.

This was going to be fun.

The downstairs apartment had fantastic potential, but needed absolutely everything doing to it; literally a magnificent shell waiting to be brought to life. The cost of that renovation wasn't going to be cheap, and separating out the water and electrics was going to add to the excitement.

"I think we need to ring Viv and cancel those plumbers," I said, tidying away the empty bottles. Thank goodness we'd found out that we had our very own water tank, before they'd started work, and billing us.

We said our *ciao ciaos* to the two men and climbed the tall stairs to bed. The next morning when we spoke to Viv, she had news.

"I was about to ring you actually," she said briskly. "There's an Australian coming to look at the coach house. He's flying in tomorrow."

"Did you know that we have our backup water tank?" Peter cut in.

There was the tiniest little pause.

"A what?"

"We don't need those plumbers and we don't need a new tank, we already have one. In the boiler room. You must have known that."

Another pause.

"I don't know what you're talking about. I'm late for a viewing. Maybe I'll see you when I show him around; his name's Ted." She rang off abruptly.

Peter stood still, holding the phone. "She knows. Did you hear her? She must've known. Probably going to get a backhander for getting those plumbers in. God, what a racket."

My stomach flopped. My mind flashed back to our first contact with Viv. We were in Wiltshire, so excited, making plans to move abroad and deciding whether or not we could put our faith in an agent overseas. There were so many things we just had to take on faith because we had no contacts in Italy. *Sometimes you just have to trust people,* we'd decided.

Well, we had. And here we were.

We were no longer those exciting people you sometimes hear about, who decide after decades of parenting to move abroad somewhere amazing and re-invent themselves. We were now those sad, disillusioned people living abroad in a house full of problems, brought on by putting faith in the hands of the wrong people.

How could we possibly have afforded a house this great on the proceeds of a little beach cottage? Well, the fact of the matter was, it was affordable for a reason.

Well, the fact of the matter was, it was affordable for a reason. We had to find a solution to everything soon. We had friends coming to visit; long-time actor friends from London. We didn't want to spend the duration of their visit moaning and complaining.

Now here's the thing; this is the deal. This is the Life Lesson I learned that day.

Taking risks is risky. I'm sure that sounds daft but it's true. For people like me – worried, anxious, fearful people – we feel that the decision to take a risk deserves a pat on the back, a gold medal. But deciding to take a risk does not alleviate you from the consequences of risk-taking; it's still risky.

I hadn't realised this. I thought that being brave was its own reward. Nothing bad was ever going to happen to us *because I was being such a good girl* choosing to take the risky, not the safe, route.

But that was just bollocks. By choosing to take the risky choice, one has to then deal with the fallout of that choice, which may – or may not – be disastrous.

I felt so stupid. And so foolish. What else was wrong with the house? And what were we going to do? Pack it all in and go back to Britain? Stay and muscle it out? Sue the hell out of everybody we could think of?

We had come here with such high hopes, craving beauty, peace, and health. But those come at a price. The beauty was also wild and untamed. The peace was periodic. And our health was beginning to suffer.

No. We just had to lie in the bed we'd made for ourselves. And figure it out.

Some might say that my decision to marry an Englishman and leave California for London was risky. Some might say that our decision to leave London for rural Wales was risky. And home educating our children. Risky. But these all were exciting choices and had a sort of protective gauze over them; nothing *really bad* was going to happen to us.

But this situation was different. We had moved lock, stock, and barrel to a foreign country, with a different language which I was struggling to learn, and we had absolutely no friends or contacts out here. We were on a retirement income until I could start my own business. We had bought, outright, a property with serious flaws. We were at risk. What were we going to do about it?

Tim and Tom should have contacted us by now. They would be in Wiltshire, packing up the remainder of our belongings for Trip Number Two. There had been a deathly silence from them which we attributed to the broken cigarette lighter. Things had been so miserable when they had arrived, neither of us wanted to really contact them and hear their gloom down the phone.

Peter rang them.

The international ring tone went.

"Hello?" Tim answered.

"Tim," Peter said, perfunctorily. "Where are you? Are you there yet?"

There was a beat.

"Uh, no. I'm in Wales."

"What?!!" Peter sat down suddenly.

"We've come straight back. I'm at my house in Denbigh."

"What the?????" Peter was floored. "Why aren't you in Wiltshire? Where's the rest of our furniture???"

The line crackled suddenly.

"I just wanted to come home." Tim's voice began to sound quavery. "I've had enough. I'm so tired. I miss my little boys; I've never been away from them for this long before. And Debbie told me I had to come home straight away or else…I had to borrow money from my brother to get across the Channel Tunnel. I'm sorry, Peter, but |I just don't want to go back there. I've had it."

I stared at Peter. I could hear most of what Tim was saying down the phone.

We had given notice on the house in Wiltshire. It was still half full of our furniture. The van we'd hired was in North Wales. And the driver too. And we were in Lazio with a crooked estate agent. What else could possibly go wrong?

Rocca d'Arce sunrise in winter

Distant view of Fontana Liri Superiore...

Fontana Liri Superiore from another angle

The Colli house (with green shutters)

Fontana Liri Superiore

The front door, Christmas 2018

Stairs and more stairs

The Colli house bedroom

Sandy snoozing at a Colli house window

The Chickens Who Came Home to Roost

We sat in the kitchen, brooding. What were we going to do? We'd just gotten here; the last thing we wanted to do was go back so soon.

Clearly we had pushed Tim too far. He was a delicate soul. I was just thinking that Tim pushed himself too far – what with going through southern Germany and all – but hindsight is a marvellous thing.

I think we had just made a plan that required a certain sort of personality, and amiable, garden-loving Tim and his mate were just not those sorts of people.

I felt like a Harridan. Sort of. And also a Victim.

In order to rectify this car crash of a scenario, somebody was going to have to get our stuff, in a van, and get across from Wiltshire to Lazio. At least the items would already be packed for international travel. But this also involved closing up our Wiltshire house, returning the keys, arranging a final clean, and guessing what size van we'd need, since of course we hadn't been party to the first move and didn't have any idea how much stuff was left. I'd actually left supper, and milk, in the 'fridge for Tim and Toms' arrival. Someone was going to have to throw out the spoiled food and defrost the fridge freezer as well.

We had already taken a large storage room in an incredibly high-end storage facility in Frome, before we'd moved abroad. I was tempted to move in there, to one of those storage rooms, if Italy didn't work out. It had a cool red and mid-grey colour scheme, nice toilets, and a little kitchenette with complimentary coffee, fresh milk and a microwave. It has all manner of specialist furniture moving trolleys, and none of them had wobbly wheels. I would have been very happy living there.

But we were in Italy. Our possessions were scattered across Lazio, Wiltshire, and North Wales. Peter finally decided that if we wanted something done right, we were jolly well going to do it ourselves. We were going to make the second journey.

Now, to be honest, although I couldn't bear leaving the house we'd just moved into – despite its inherent problems – I had a tiny little voice deep inside of me which I was trying not to listen to. It was calling out for my children. I didn't want to listen to this little voice because it made absolutely no rational sense to move to a foreign country and then complain about missing your children.

But I did. Miss them. Maybe they were growing up, but I wasn't.

So despite my external objections I was secretly coming 'round to the idea in record time. I could see my children. We could get our stuff. We'd buy Lottery tickets along the way – and win – and spend our fortune renovating the house. Everything would be okay. And then I could knuckle down and start doing the work I'd set out to do when I moved there.

I suggested going at half term when both boys would be free. We would deal with the get-out at the Wiltshire house, move our belongings from the nice storage facility (sob) to a less expensive container site in a little field near Bath, and if need be, put overflow items which wouldn't fit in the van, into it as well.

This would allow me to unpack the myriad boxes we still had sloping around the Colli house and make room for the second load. It was all becoming clear.

Sometimes in life you just have periods of times where you have to do *shit jobs*. Moving house. Clearing gutters. Spring cleaning. Hoovering your car interior. Raking leaves. Sorting your attic. Sorting your basement. We were coming up to one of those times. But the joy of seeing our boys, and the excitement of driving across Western Europe again, sweetened the deal considerably.

Miraculously, Peter found an Italian van hire company that would allow a driver in his late seventies to drive out of the country and over to England, with a wife and a dog. For anyone who has ever hired a van you will appreciate that not everybody is so *laissez-faire* with their vans. It is the Italian way. I couldn't drive a stick-shift so it was down to Peter to do all the driving.

We were really broke by this time so we decided to crash with friends and family during the journey. I always prefer hotels because I really hate imposing on people by staying over, especially with a dog in tow, but we have an amazing network of people in this country so we were very graciously received.

We really couldn't schedule any improvements to the house because we were just about to leave again, so I just had to bide my time and extract as much enjoyment out of our situation as I could.

It actually went rather well. For the most part.

We left Rome in a thundery downpour, me stressing wildly about leaving our own car parked on the street while we took the van abroad. I hate that feeling when you climb into a rental vehicle, and you settle down inside, check out whether or not it's a nice vehicle, or a crappy vehicle, and then you set off on your merry way. We pulled away from the curb, Sandy settled comfortably by my side, Peter stalling occasionally as he re-acquainted himself with stick-shift driving. I then really, fully realized that we were going to be in this vehicle, for a very long time: a stick-shift rental van, all the way from Rome to Wiltshire and back. It was time to put on my Big Girls Pants and be very, very brave indeed.

JOURNAL ENTRY

We have just returned from a fortnight away, driving in an Italian rental van to collect more furniture from the U.K.

Driving, in Italy, is an *Alpha Experience*.

Having established the nature of our fellow drivers here, I need to describe the roads. The Autostrada are well maintained, and slick, and although they are dotted with tolls, you can see just outside your window the result of these tolls, as roadworks continually maintain the surfaces, and are kept to the verge whenever possible to ensure minimal disruption to passing cars. We experienced some curious anomalies during our travels — a ticket dispenser out of ink, for example — but in general the system seems to work well.

But: if the system breaks down, it is a vision of hell...

As we travelled up into France, we needed to choose a route to take us from our new home in Frosinone region, south of Rome. I didn't use to have a problem with tunnels, but after my sister-in-law's hair-raising description of a journey through the Monte Blanc tunnel, I began to develop tunnel issues.

As a result, we decided to avoid the Monte Blanc and

so chose a different route, via Turin, to take us into France. It was pretty, and dramatic, and a challenging drive, and every time we came to a tunnel I would look down, or shut my eyes, and think of other things. The length of the tunnels are always marked on a sign at the mouth of the tunnel, but I decided that this was not helpful information, and so I decided that channelling thoughts of a jacuzzi experience in a tropical resort was a far healthier way of focussing my concentration.

We seemed to be ascending, endlessly, towards the French border, and although our (empty) van was coping well, I wondered how happy the vehicle would be when we were heavily laden, on our return journey. I saw the mouth of another tunnel approaching, and dutifully closed my eyes. My husband pulled the van up to a toll booth and gasped as the machine recorded a toll demand for 123.00 Euros. We paid it and carried on, wondering how we could afford lunch after a toll like that. We entered the tunnel, and I felt an uncomfortable rush of pressure on my inner ear. The sounds around us changed imperceptibly, and I suddenly got a tingling feeling that this was no ordinary tunnel. My heart began to pound, and I started to chatter, maniacally, about I can't remember what, and I could hear lorries charging past us, small cars streaking past us, and fear imbedding itself deeply in my nervous system.

The tunnel went on, and on, and on. Ugly images cut

across my mental, tropical escape route, slashing through my jacuzzi thoughts and blossoming into a migraine. I could hear the regular throb of the road underneath us, and see through my closed eyelids the artificial brightness that was the tunnel lighting, a grim reminder that we were not in broad daylight, but in fact deep underground.

Just as I thought I couldn't take any more, the pressure began to release from my ears. It was nine minutes of hell, and 123.00 Euros for the privilege. At the next rest stop, over a frugal bun and espresso, we agreed that the return journey would be through the more placid roads of southern France towards the sea, and not through the mountains.

Things were fairly quiet for a time. It was dark by now, and the red winking lights of the Industrial North were floating high up into the night sky. The road to Bologna/Milan was flat and unambitious. After what seemed to be an endless route we turned off from Bologna.

And then the tunnels began.

We were exhausted. I mean, truly, bone-weary, nerve-shattered, aching, hungry, depleted.

My sat-nav began to flag up "Road Works" symbols. Gargantuan lorries, frustrated at our timidity, bullied past us, blasting their horns and jockeying for position in front of us. I wasn't quite sure of the wisdom of honking your horn at someone who was already travelling in the slow lane, but things had gotten past the reasonable stage and were now into the realm of the extreme, the unreasonable, the outrageous.

The tunnels and the roadworks began to flare up with grim regularity. I couldn't escape to my tropical jacuzzi anymore, as I was required to decipher the symbols on the Sat-Nav. Time flexed and straightened and distorted itself beyond all recognition. My husband was flagging, it was now early in the morning. The sights and sounds were nightmarish: speeding vehicles, manic flashing lights, small lanes, pressure all around us.

Tunnel after tunnel after tunnel assaulted us, at high speed, hemmed in by single lanes and road works and edgy aggressive drivers threatening annihilation at every bend. My head was aching, my throat was tight from suppressed sobs, I gripped the phone with one hand and the door handle with the other, in a white-knuckle vice grip.

Finally, somewhere around Florence, we cut off the road into a slim layby, packed with giant lorries and sleeping drivers. My husband closed his eyes and was instantly asleep, crumpled into the corner of the cab, snoring gently. Every nerve in my body was jarred, and I ached in so many different places, it all joined together into one enormous mass of discomfort. I curled myself into the other end of the cab, struggling to find comfort somewhere, and finding none. Out of the left side of the van, ghoulish bright lights from the road works danced between the skipping high-speed lights of the passing lorries. I don't know why the engines screamed as they passed, but they did. Out of the right side of the cab there was a steep ravine, delving down into blackness, city lights winking, in the distance, and pine trees bending mournfully above me.

Honeymoon Phase

My plan, once we'd settled in Colli, was to write. Perhaps cater. Maybe run a cookery school. I was a bit vague about the details, because I was wise enough to be patient and check out the lay of the land there first before embarking on a career. I did feel though, that I should be in Italy and involved in the food industry in some way. The blog posts were fun to write and people back in Britain seemed interested in what I was posting.

I thought maybe I could offer cookery courses for tourists. We were equidistant between Naples and Roma, perfect for a stopover, a couple of nights and a swim at Ville del Colle, and a few sessions on Italian cookery. The Americans would love it, and of course the British market too.

But the more settled we got into the community, and the more I began to understand the nature of where I was, the more I realised I had to throw my business plan out and start again.

I didn't speak Italian. I was having a terrible time with the language. And frankly, even if I did speak Italian, everyone around me spoke it better. Running any sort of business here without a full working knowledge of the language was going to be a disaster.

And why would anyone want to travel all the way across from America to be taught Italian cookery by an American? It just wasn't authentic. I discovered quite soon that there was already a cookery school in Rocca d'Arce, fifteen minutes away. And they were Italian. They had a wonderful setup already, with accommodation, and a big space for classes.

How could I run any sort of business relating to food if I didn't have a reliable source of water? And if I did run a business from our new home, which involved people coming to the house, where were they going to park? There was already a jostling competition each day for parking spaces nearest the square. If you came back late at night you had to park further down the steep slope at the bottom of the square, and schlep up, in all weathers.

And the location of our little village, despite its convenient situation between the two major cities, was very quiet, very rural, and didn't have the major tourist attractions which people were so keen to see on their holidays. I could find delight in the waterfalls at Isola de Liri, or the beaded jewels of light atop the little hill towns at sunset, but they were nothing compared with the Coliseum, or Pompeii, or the gondolas of Venice. Our neighbourhood was the sort of place that wealthy Romans would visit for a bit of country charm, but only if you were in the mood for simplicity. And if I was catering for the American and British markets, I would need to find more people out here who were bi-lingual.

Reluctantly I abandoned my idea of creating a business which involved having people come and stay. If people came here on holiday, there were other businesses which did that sort of work better than me. And they were Italian.

I decided that writing was really the best way forward: send my stories and my blogs and my photos back home to the U.K. If you weren't in a position to travel to Italy on holiday, at least vicariously you could feel like you had.

So I carried on with my journal, working title ITALY UNDER GLASS, describing the little everyday adventures which made up the lives of the residents of this tiny village.

JOURNAL ENTRY EXTRACTS

CATS AND DOGS

Once back in the street on the way home, there are cats and dogs draped carelessly about in the lane. These animals are street-smart. The cats, for the most part, are louche and lean. They shift about quietly under cars and windowsills with their heads hunkered low, looking for trouble. Once I encountered one in a friend's back terrace, caramel-coloured and cruel. It had designs on my shopping bag, but was waved on smartly by my hostess. It squatted malevolently, preparing to propel a hairball in my direction, but lost courage and darted away into the bushes, empty-handed.

The dogs are far more congenial and boisterous. The pocket-sized dogs are used to being coddled and kissed and tucked into oversized handbags on market day. They offered little resistance to wherever they are placed: on a lap, in a basket, on the bonnet of a car, on the sill at the local post office. The larger dogs vie for dominance. Down our lane, a jet-black mongrel with a fiercesome temper bays madly, and spins round on its own axis behind a grim fence. When you coo at it and say "Ooh, you don't scare me, little one!" it spins faster, barks louder, and threatens to implode. A flabby-cheeked boxer lives on the roof terrace a bit further down. It spits barks down at the passers-by from its eyrie two floors up. I suspect it would dissolve into a puddle of cuddles were you to climb the stairs to the top and present it with a tempting tidbit.

Next door lives a tiny black chihuahua. It is the beloved small pet of a simple, joyful young lad. It is a fickle little beast, sometimes turning on its adoring owner for no good reason, and having not a kind word to say to anybody else, neither man nor beast. It seems to be one of those animals that deeply resents being small. It challenges anyone who comes near, regardless of size. I think were it to be allowed down from its owner's loving arms, it would chase you down the lane, and tattoo you sharply with its tiny teeth, somewhere just above the ankle.

BINS

The rubbish recycling system is great here, if a little unreliable. There is a different collection each weekday morning, which is bliss after our Britain experience, where fortnightly recycling schemes are the norm, (and I understand that three-weekly collections are in the offing). Also, in our village, the recycling is done at a civilised time of the morning, rather than at the crack of dawn as in Britain, which is really a help because with the temperamental weather here you really don't want to put anything out the night before and run the risk of it flying all over the street before sunrise. There are separate days for plastics, glass, cardboard and paper, organic waste, and metal. My favourite is the "Household" collection day. I haven't had this thoroughly explained to me, but I get the impression that it is a day for anything you have missed during the previous week, and anything you can't categorise. A teabag, for example, is made up of biological material (tea leaves), paper (tea bag), and metal (the staple). I saw an elderly ironing board put out recently with an impressive display of burn marks on it, and even a few holes. It was there in the morning and gone by the afternoon. I assume that the Household collection came to the rescue. I was very generous with my Household recycling collection yesterday morning, and it all went, but this morning my glass and biological offerings were ignored, and sat there slightly steaming in the hot sun as we returned home from market. I have no idea why.

We were incredibly lucky, actually; they took all of our packing boxes. Every single one. There must have been about 200. Every cardboard recycling day, we would make a large pile of collapsed packing boxes outside our door and they would be magically spirited away by lunchtime.

SECRETS

In the spirit of full disclosure, and in order to accurately represent our experience here in Italy, I must reveal to you in all sincerity that there is something wrong with the house. I mean, I know I've mentioned the carefree shutters, and the dubious plumbing, and the whimsical irregularity of the recycling. But to be honest I've been putting a brave face on things, as I'm in the first flush of love with this house, and young newlyweds always turn a blind eye to foibles and imperfections in each other; such is the power of love.

The moving, and the plans, the schedules and the lists and charts and calendars and coordination of it all had kept us busy and our minds occupied; I had no time to reflect or brood. But the morning I woke up, felt the first of the morning's autumnal chill air, and stumbled through the war zone that was our front hall in search of coffee, I began to feel really lonely.

I felt a bit sick. I could almost hear the distance between us and the country we'd left, feel the oceans and the continents separating us from a country filled with our friends and family, and familiar trees, plants, foods, sounds, smells, architecture, humour, and of course, language. We were here now, in a picture postcard of Italy, but it was a postcard filled with people not yet friends, and places not yet familiar. I missed my boys intensely.

Autumn was creeping silently up the valley, and as the days began to get shorter, the temperatures dropped. Our little terrace was still, daily, a Mediterranean sun trap, but indoors the thick, cool walls of summer took on a heavy chill once the sun went down, and stayed cold throughout the night.

Gone now were the strappy sandals, the sunblock, the filmy tee shirts and loose linen trousers. Whatever the weather was outside — and so often it was fine — the house began to rebel against us and exude a deeply cold and head-achingly icy atmosphere.

CENTRAL HEATING

You could walk into a chilled and stony room, bare feet stabbed by the icy stone floors, and if you placed your hand on a radiator it was scalding, but the heat just seemed to evaporate within inches of the radiator. After a few weeks of trying to heat the entire house, my husband calculated that it would cost roughly 245 euros a week to keep to central heating running every room, and we hastily decided to close down most of the house and pick our heating battles carefully.

The choice was this: either close down the entire top floor, or the entire bottom floor, to conserve energy. We finally agreed to close down all heating on the ground floor and create a little bedsit for ourselves upstairs.

The splendid long bedroom we had created for ourselves suited this perfectly: it accommodated a large bed, a breakfast table and chairs, and two comfortable upholstered armchairs in front of the pink marble fireplace. Adjacent to this room we had created a small dressing room, lined with wardrobes and dressers, and connected to the dressing room was the bathroom. A very small corridor became a small breakfast kitchen, with fridge, toaster, cafetières, and the like. Through the kitchenette was the lounge, and further on, my husband's office. We confined ourselves to this long apartment, carrying electric heaters and gas stoves from room to room as needed. The views from this eyrie were spectacular, scenes of snow-capped mountains in the distance and sunrises bursting out pink, orange and gold each morning.

We had virtually no visitors at all to the house, save Theresa's weekly visits. Each time she was scheduled to clean I would turn on the central heating, in a feeble attempt to warm the place for her. I felt so embarrassed: the house was so cold and we looked so impoverished, bedecked in woolly jumpers and scarves, corralled as we were in a mere one third of our actual available living space. She politely declined to notice the glacial atmosphere. She always arrived, smiling, armed with a soft woollen jumper and scarf, which was soon discarded as she set to work, working up a sweat as she cleaned the house and mopped the acres of cold stone floors in this vast, 17th century ice sculpture.

We all stopped for an espresso break halfway through her visits. My husband and I were usually to be found thawing out on the terracotta terrace, shedding our winter wraps as the sun beat down on us, watching the pale olivewood smoke curling across the rooftops from our neighbours' chimneys.

SILENCE

I usually love silence. I crave peaceful dawns, and pastoral sunsets. This is not Italian, or at least not where we live. There is so much life in this valley, and it is all happening simultaneously, and at great volume. Pigeons, owls, goats and their kids, dogs, sheep, children, police klaxons, builders rumbling, church bells, lorries, housewives and househusbands...

LIGHTBULBS 1

I have begun to worry about the lightbulbs. There are fifty lightbulbs, in total, throughout the house, and those are just the ones in the ceiling lights. That doesn't include desk lamps, reading lamps, standard lamps, two wall sconces, the bulbs in the refrigerators, and the burnt-out bulb in the extractor fan over the oven that doesn't work. The lightbulbs have begun to go. Assuming they were all put in at the same time, they probably will begin to go at the same time as well.

50 lightbulbs at let's say €2.50 each, equals €125.00 for lightbulbs alone. And then there will be the cost of the tall, A-frame ladder, to reach the lights. At a guess, the chandelier in the stairwell is probably fifteen feet high, and the ones in the office and lounge are probably ten feet high, and the other hall and kitchen lights are well over eight feet as well. And then when I am up my newly purchased tall A-frame ladder I will see the dust on the lampshades, casting a slightly murky taupe-like haze over the brilliance of the bulb, and I will want to give the lampshades a bit of a wash. This may take some time. I could ask Theresa to do them, but if she begins, she may ultimately be late for the ringing of the noontime church bells.

LIGHTBULBS 2

...The lightbulbs have begun to go. I had feared that they would all go at the same time, but luckily they seem to be staggering their departures. There was a promisingly tall ladder here when we viewed the house but this has disappeared, and we have to determine just how many bulbs will go before we need to borrow a ladder and tackle the problem.

To their credit, the previous owners left everything single bulb working when they left, so it is only recently that we have had this problem. We are in that awkward period where tungsten bulbs are being phased out and the newer, energy efficient bulbs — with their blue-grey tinge — are being phased in. There are, apparently, warmer yellow energy efficient bulbs if you can find them, but the colder, bluer lights seem to be most available in the High streets.

Things were getting precarious in the high, vaulted kitchen, with only one working bulb left, so we finally asked to borrow a ladder from Teresa, and set about taking out the burnt bulbs. My husband had scaled our own small, tinny, English ladder and had plummeted to the floor, smashing the antique glass shade and narrowly missing a sharp-edged furniture piece on his way down. It was a heart-stopping moment, and I panicked, envisaging this happening fifty times over every time a bulb went. Teresa's ladder was taller, and stronger, encrusted in years of paint, and better equipped to deal with the tall ceilings.

Neighbours

Ted was a real live wire. He didn't so much enter a room as tear it apart. I think he was what you might call a Force of Nature (not really sure what that means, actually), or a Real Character. The key feature to remember about Ted is that he was a good guy. Underneath all of the bluster, and Alpha personality, he was a tender soul who loved his girlfriend dearly and had a dream of converting this Italian coach house into his own personal Xanadu.

Ted had the personality to take risks, unlike me. It was interesting to watch a dyed-in-the-wool risk taker do battle with the likes of Viv and Mario. He brushed aside small talk about "how was your flight?" and "how was Australia.?" He was completely focussed on the house. He'd bought it. From Viv. We hadn't had a chance to meet him and talk to him – Viv had made sure of that – and he'd gone ahead and bought it.

"*Let me show you what I'm gonna do*," he said, passionately, steaming down the fragile narrow steps to his new lair. We struggled to keep up. We'd seen the coach house briefly when we had viewed our own house, and I had loved the impossibly tall windows, big chunky wooden doors, the overgrown terraced garden, the two-storey vaulted ceiling.

Ted was smitten as well.

"We're gonna put a swimming pool there", he gestured outside to one of the long tiers of the terraced garden. "Fruit trees here" he pointed excitedly. "I'm going to build a scaffold up to a mezzanine floor and have the bedroom up here. Here's the kitchen, and the bathroom will go here." He was waving his arms, but not wildly, it was very focussed and with great energy. It was impossible not to get caught up in his enthusiasm.

"A pool?" Peter said, admiringly. "That's impressive."

We glanced at each other. Water. In order to have a pool you need to have water. Where was that going to come from? What had Viv told him about the situation between the two houses? Obviously not much or I doubt he would have bought it.

There was no plumbing installed in his place so we decided to worry about it later. He'd be back at some point and we'd hash it out then. Off he went to his plane, no doubt making it airborne with his personality alone and sending it shooting off towards Australia.

We decided the time had come to meet our neighbour with the hoover. We had friends coming over soon and we needed to start separating out our utilities. Jaka arranged to translate an introduction. He didn't like her much. Apparently she talked a mile a minute and never let you put a word in edgewise. I was not looking forward to this meeting.

Graziella came to the front door of the house, a tiny little bird of a woman with a fur-collared coat. She was perfectly coiffed, made up, manicured, in the best Italian manner. Although she was petite in stature she drew herself up to her full height and extracted every inch she could.

Jaka filled us in on her background. She had been widowed fairly recently. Her late husband had taken care of the management of the household and now she was out of her depth, dealing with new neighbours, strangers in her boiler room, and the possibility of a mad Australian installing a swimming pool below her bedroom window. Life must have changed drastically for her in a short space of time and she was handling it as best she could. I thought about her each morning as I sat on the terrace with my morning coffee, hearing the hoover whining back and forth. I had never heard of anyone hoovering their house every single morning; that was hotel behaviour. I wondered if maybe I was the odd one, only deigning to hoover when there had been a spill of some sort, or people were visiting, or I woke up in an unusual mood.

I pictured in my imagination her home: acres of marble floors, gleaming, clean and smooth, inherited antiques everywhere, perhaps the gentle ticking of an heirloom clock on the mantlepiece. Somewhere prominent there would be a Madonna and child – she was very devout – and Catholic relics would be placed over the headboards of the beds in every room. There would be a shrine, and votives. Perhaps there might be a decanter of something reviving, made of crystal, and a hostess trolley. She wasn't a florid Italian, she was an upright Italian.

We gestured for her to come in and she stepped across the doorway, staring into the airy hallway as if she had not been there for years. Jaka explained to her what we had discovered; that there were things which her brother and husband should have separated out but hadn't.

She started to fluster. She wouldn't look us in the eye and barely acknowledged us; she only spoke with Jaka. He finished his explanation. She managed to extract one more half inch from her delicate frame and then she attacked. The volley of rapid-fire Italian hit us, Jaka, the walls, the ceiling; it was everywhere.

She didn't want anyone in her boiler room. She didn't want anyone near her water supply. She didn't want anyone near the electricity box. She didn't want anyone coming down to the pass door into the basement level. It was her private property and belonged to her family and no strangers were allowed in. The Australian would not be allowed access to his new house through her pass door, he would have to go down the exterior steps no matter what the weather was like. The parking space outside her door was hers and hers alone. This information was all hurled at Jaka like a volley of arrows; we were merely onlookers.

Jaka looked helplessly at us and briefly translated, leaving out a few of the choicer remarks, I suspect. Peter countered, stating that we had purchased the property with access to our utilities and were entitled to have access to maintain them. He held up the enormous tangle of keys and said to Jaka that they had been handed to us personally by Lucio, on the day we had exchanged contracts. He daren't mention having the diesel delivered; that was going to be fun.

She erupted again, before Jaka could finish the translation. Things were escalating faster than we had ever imagined. I could only think that she had been sitting up there in her noble apartment, frightened, angry, helpless, not knowing how to handle the situation, not knowing who to turn to, and building an armoury of weapons with which to defend herself.

I was reminded slightly of the Tasmanian devil in the Looney Tunes cartoons, whirling with anger and resentment. We looked uncomfortably at Jaka and decided amongst ourselves that we should try a different tack. On a different day. Using different people.

She stalked out and up the lane, marching in her trim little Italian leather shoes across the cobblestones. We had hoped that we could separate the electrics and the water so we could make as few trips as possible to the smelly little room downstairs, but we were going to have to give her a wide berth in order to do so. Every time the fuses blew Peter would trudge downstairs and reset them. Nobody wanted to be down there.

The next morning, the combination of kettle and clothes washer blew the fuses. My mistake. Peter dutifully set off to the boiler room with his keys. He returned quicker than I'd expected, looking grim.

"She's locked the door. She's gone and locked the door into the downstairs passage." Peter had described to me a thick bolt and bar across the door which were quite brutal, could catch your fingers if you weren't careful. These had been put to use, not to repel Barbarians, but to repel the outside world, including us. "We have no electrics until I can get into that room."

I looked at my watch. Half nine. I didn't think Jaka would be up much before eleven, as it was a weekend, so we had to make coffee on the stove and sit quietly outside until we could get our electricity back. Peter finally gingerly crept across the lane and knocked tentatively, not knowing what to expect.

Jaka came to the door, with a bedhead. He looked wearily at Peter and reached for his shoes. The men disappeared up the lane and I stayed in the front door, watched the morning sky, shimmering with morning sun. Everything was quiet. No arguing, no chatting, no laughter. Silence.

I went back into the kitchen and waited nervously at the table.

Within the space of ten minutes they were back, Jaka looking a bit worse for wear. Peter was tight lipped.

"Electricity's back on. Everything's fine. For now. We threatened to ring the police."

I stared at them both, trying to tell if the encounter had been amicable. I gathered not.

Peter took a sip of his cold coffee and looked up at the black widow spider of a chandelier, coiled above us in the dining room.

"This is not going to be easy," he predicted.

We didn't have much time to bemoan our lot in life because we had work to do. We were expecting house guests. We had done our best to make the house safe, comfortable, and reliable, but there was only so much we could do without engaging in the major refurbishments we were bracing ourselves for.

They duly arrived, flying into Naples airport. They were so excited, just being in Italy, and being the first guests in our new home. We felt so jaded – what with everything going wrong and all – that it was really refreshing to show them around and rediscover the joy which had first taken us there.

We continued to have problems with the house – sort of like a subterranean rumble under everything we did – but having friends to stay sort of felt like a protection against things getting really, truly awful.

BLOG POST: THE (FAILED) ASCENT OF ROCCA D'ARCE

Rocca d'Arce greets me every morning: tall, angular, and imposing in the early Italian light. It's only about twenty minutes from our house. Everything about it is deceptive. From my bedroom window it looks distant and wildly majestic, somewhat dwarfed by the mountain range behind it. The closer we get to it the taller it becomes, and frankly more suburban.

At the foot of Rocca d'Arce lies the small town of Arce, a pocket-sized watering hole for visitors travelling through the Liri river valley on their way to the A1 trunk route from Rome to Naples. There are many shops, cafes, and bars in Arce, modest and accommodating. But as you pass through the town there is a constant impulse to crane your neck and peer upwards towards the top of the ragged peak.

It's actually impossible to see the summit of Rocca d'Arce from the valley floor. It shoots upwards and then leans back on itself, shielding the upper third of the mountain behind scrub brush and cliff-hanging apartment blocks.

When our London friends came to visit we challenged them with a visit to, and ascent of, Rocca d'Arce. From the relative safety of our terrace, over a glass of Campari and orange, this seemed like a splendid idea.

Our sat-nav has two voices. One we have dubbed the rather diffident "Clive", and the other, the long-suffering "Amy". Clive has a rather dubious hold on the Italian language, and announces "Make a U-turn and proceed to the route" whenever we go wrong. Amy, on the other hand, goes to great lengths to avoid criticising us when we take a wrong turn. In fact, she never corrects our driving choices, but amiably takes us miles out of our way in search of an alternative route, no matter how scenic or long-winded it may be.

On the occasion of The Ascent of Rocca d'Arce Amy was in charge. We did in fact go wrong somewhat early into our journey, blithely sailing past a blue road sign very clearly pointing to ROCCA D'ARCE off to the left. True to form, Amy did not ask us to go back on ourselves but took us on a breath-taking journey up into the foothills of the Rocca d'Arce slopes. Sheer rainwater gullies were sliced into the cliff on either side of the road; hairpin bends led us straight into the path of oncoming, road-hogging Minis. Impatient non-descript European cars tailgated us from behind. Which was worse: carrying on up the ever-diminishing mountain tracks towards the summit (and certain death), or making a hair-raising three-point-turn in the middle of the tiny road, avoiding gullies and oncoming cars, to descend again to the valley floor?

Some of us clutched the arm rests. Some of us clutched the seat backs in front of us. Some of us closed our eyes. Amazingly, we began to descend, to the dulcet tones of Amy, gently urging us onwards.

We blindly followed Amy into a gentle, fertile valley, edged on either side with half-finished holiday villas and acres of verdant farmland. There were mountains behind us, mountains in front of us, and miles of farmland in between. We passed villages with delightful names like Colfelice ("happy hill"). The tall craggy peak and radio masts of Rocca d'Arce slowly disappeared behind us. Getting lost never seemed so appealing.

At last we shut down the sat-nav, and relied on common sense and intuition to get us back on track, ascending again up the sheer slopes. After several red-herring roads and cliff-hanger moments, we curled around one final bend and suddenly the road opened gracefully onto a long, wide, sunny piazza, lined with shady trees, fountains, a softly fading avenue of shops, and an enormous church. We seemed to have been travelling ever-upwards and I expected to see the radio masts and the summit at every turn. When we finally got out of our cars and looked up we discovered that we were barely one third of the way up the mountain side. Never had so much effort accomplished so little.

I'm uncertain how such a steep cliff could afford space for such a generous town centre, but you would never know from walking down the centre of the street how high up you were. It was tranquil: a shady café offered tables and espresso, the commanding church offered solace through enormous doors, a rather incongruous silver Bentley gleamed in the hot sun.

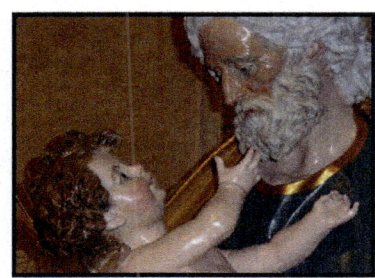 

Chiesi di SS Pietro e Paolo dominated the piazza, confident, stern, welcoming. Inside, a feast of graceful and delicate sculptures vied for my attention with works of art and architectural filigree. It was incredibly moving.

As is so often the case, getting lost whetted our appetite for lunch, but the café didn't serve food and there didn't seem to be anything else available in the street. Our friend flagged down a local youth and asked him for a lunch recommendation. Having no English at all, and our Italian being just as non-existent, we were very grateful when he hopped in his car and drove us down the hill to show us a local restaurant.

Each morning I still wake up to the pastel vision that is Rocca d'Arce. I squint to see the spot, one third of the way up the side, where we were foiled in our ascent. I have plans to go back; the gauntlet is still thrown down. But I will be older, and wiser, and in possession of a map and a sedative. It is my personal Everest, and it remains to be conquered.

———————————————————————

Not Everybody Was Out to Get us

Amongst all of the skulduggery and trauma we were experiencing with our house, we met some truly delightful people. Kind people. People who had a sort of generous and amiable outlook on life which I myself have never been able to achieve, but I so value it in others. Is it an Italian personality trait? Is it rural? Faith-based? I've no idea. Kind people can be found the world over, ducking and weaving carefully amongst the rotters. Here are a few of my favourites.

Petrol Station Guy

Within our first week in Colli we went to the local self-serve, unattended petrol station in the centre of the village. Peter duly put his credit card into the slot on the pump and plugged in 50.00 Euros. Nothing happened. The money had been taken but no petrol came out. Baffled, and slightly alarmed, he went next door to the local shop and mimed his experience to Sophia, the shop owner. She looked alarmed and came out into the street, miming back with great enthusiasm, that "The station, it has been closed some time. There is no petrol."

Peter gestured the sign for money, and shrugged a question. Sophia's partner came out, full of authority, waving vaguely off down the lower street of the town towards the river.

"*Stazione di servizio,*" he proclaimed, proudly solving our petrol problem but not our money problem.

We thanked him and took off, driving slowly and carefully, as our tank was dangerously low. After a bit of a wander, we found a modestly sized petrol station, with attached café and self-serve car wash. Next door to it we could just see the tops of an elegant Italian house, surrounded by lush gardens.

A kindly man ambled out, luckily having some English. Peter half-mimed, half-spoke his predicament, the Italian man listening carefully to his tale. He glanced across to me and acknowledged me with a smile, smiled at Sandy in the back seat.

"I will help you", he said quietly, gesturing to his petrol pump. "The Colli petrol station, it is closed. My station is of the same company, so you please to fill your tank. I tell the company and they pay me back the money you have spent."

Peter looked dumbfounded, at this trusting, thoughtful soul. We always went there for our petrol after that. After each visit, Peter would emerge with some little gift or treat from the owner. Once he had fresh sun-warmed peaches from his lovely garden. Another time it was a tin of excellent Italian coffee. In the next door café you could pay your utility bills, and as you waited for the transaction to be processed there was always a cup of espresso, gratis, while you waited. It raised the act of selling petrol to some sort of incredibly civilised, elegant transaction.

He and his son were also the lucky folk who we asked to lug large heavy metal cans of diesel oil down into our boiler room lair, risking the wroth of Graziella in the process.

Il Dottore, The Doctor

In Italy, the distinctions between many things are blurred. Take the doctor, for example. Qualified as a doctor, he also performed dentistry. Now you'd think, if you came from America or England, that dentistry was so specialised a profession that a doctor couldn't learn everything about medicine as well as everything about dentistry. But in Italy this was possible. Lucio, the previous house owner, had been the local doctor/dentist and, although he had status in the village by dint of noble birth and profession, I had the impression that though respected he was not necessarily liked.

This doctor was different. He looked like a Doctor of Philosophy for a start, erudite, sociable, thick wavy grey Italian hair, worn longer than you'd expect. He had just enough English to understand us. He was a doctor by profession but *he lived for food*, although he was slim and of a modest stature. When on the few occasions we came to see him, we spent maybe five minutes talking symptoms, and twenty minutes talking restaurants. We would emerge from his treatment room after one of these conversations to find the once-empty waiting room now full of people, waiting patiently to be seen. They didn't seem to mind that we had been socialising on the other side of the door. When it was their turn, they too would have opportunity to provide their restaurant reviews, and perhaps he might pick up the phone and book a table at his nephew's riverfront restaurant for seven o'clock that evening, as he did for us. Never the lecture about cholesterol, or the benefits of exercise, or units of alcohol, it was all about the love of fine wines and fine dining.

I went to him to have a tooth extracted. A filling I'd had done in England came apart in Italy, and the only solution was to pull it. It's difficult to describe the terror of having a tooth extracted by someone who barely understands English. My mime skills were florid. He was momentarily piqued at the sight of a few spots of my blood on his pristine white coat. He was a dapper man.

The Veterinarian We Never Met

She was a local legend. A woman with animal husbandry skills which transcended the ordinary. Sandy needed a renewal of her extensive medications, and we were not allowed to have them sent in bulk from Britain. We needed to have a local vet take Sandy on their books and prescribe her treatment.

The vet did not take appointments. She had particular hours on particular days, and if you queued and she had to close at the end of the day you had to come back again the next morning, risking losing your place in the process. We drove to her modest building, spread out in an orchard. From the road we could see how long the queue was. The luckiest people sat on benches near the entrance, the not-quite-so-lucky sat on the low wall next to the benches, the not-nearly-as-lucky sat in their cars under the shady trees, and the impatient strolled aimlessly about the dusty car park, glaring at their watches. For the most part, people were serene. People chatted to each other, petting their dogs or their cats or their rabbits. A lone man slowly walked his horse up and down the drive. The sun beat down. Small children fidgeted. A lone fly buzzed. It could for all the world be customers waiting to be seated in a café.

Never one to wait patiently, I panicked that we would not be seen, the surgery would close, and we would have to show up at the crack of dawn the next morning in an attempt to beat the traffic and get a seat by the door. Jaka told us something amazing: veterinary prescriptions could be filled at the local pharmacy. I think the idea was that many human medicines were also suitable for animal use. We ended up filling our dog prescriptions at the Colli pharmacy, in the same building as *Il Dottore*.

Chestnut Guy

Not only do the Italians love food, they love celebrating food. Throughout the year different regional products are elevated to the level of sainthood and had festivals in their own right. One such celebration was of chestnuts. One of Antoinette's leave-behind items was an item which turned out to be a chestnut roaster, a lightweight, long-handled pan with holes cut into the bottom. It seemed incredibly Dickensian, roasting chestnuts on an open fire and all that, but I had limited resources in my kitchen.

One of our local supermarkets was Decco in Monte San Giovanni Campano. I think it might have been a family run franchise. Or perhaps the employees all really enjoyed each other's company. It was always a convivial atmosphere in there, whenever we went in.

But one day as I was trawling around the fruit and veg section I saw an enormous display of chestnuts, and a sign in Italian which I couldn't decipher. As I was staring at the sign, a tall, slender young man appeared at my side. He asked me something in Italian and I did my traditional "I don't speak Italian" shrug. His face lit up and he reached into his back pocket for his phone. He tapped away briefly – I assumed he was going for Google Translate – but he suddenly passed the phone into my hand and pressed play. It was a video, in English, about how to roast chestnuts. I stood there, in the middle of this supermarket, learning about chestnuts. It was so kind, so thoughtful. So fun.

Owner of the Agro Tourismo

Maria was like a big human hug. Warm, friendly, funny, speaking English with an American accent. She ran *Il Ciclope*, an agro tourismo in Arpino, city of culture. *Agro Tourismo* is a scheme whereby a working farm can benefit from providing accommodation and hospitality to travellers to supplement their farming income. She would arrive at your table and discuss the food of the day.

"What would you like to eat? Would you like maybe, some pasta, or we have also some lovely wild mushrooms in risotto. Maybe you would like only a main course and a dessert? We make our dishes pretty big."

No menu, no fuss, no bother. We had been introduced to her by Viv and Mario, who had taken us to lunch, along with some business acquaintances from Britain. Somehow she managed to be friends with everybody, even people who were not friends with each other. You will see photos of her terrace in the blog post AN ITALIAN MEAL. Lunches at Il Ciclope place were all day affairs, drowsy-making, under the ancient, gnarled olive trees, hearing the buzz of insects in the lavender, in the heat. One of the businessmen was so enamoured of the meal, he forgot that he was flying back to the U.K. that afternoon and missed his flight.

The Pet Boarder

Margherita loved dogs. She had cherry red hair, and a tender heart. We boarded Sandy with her on a few occasions, in her own home.

When we first looked around her facilities we could tell it would be ideal. There was a large grassy area for several dogs to play, and at night Sandy was allowed to sleep on a low Victorian daybed in the sitting room, perfectly suited to her age and gentility. Margherita was actively involved in rescuing stray dogs, which were a painful sight to see everywhere on the roads in Italy.

Fitting in

I felt sure that there must be a British ex-pat community somewhere about, but perhaps they were more likely to congregate further north in Tuscany and Perugia. We came across a handful of British-born residents when we attended a mandolin concert in Arpino, performed in an exquisite, ancient, frescoed, historic palazzo. I fully expected that we would soon become part of this community, but somehow we remained set apart. The houses in Arpino were refined, and the entire ambience of the place was elegant and cool. Arpino was spread like butter across two precarious hilltops, and the views from every angle were staggering. Colli, although blessed with views just as dramatic, was a more countrified village, with its low, sturdy, sensible buildings, built for practicality more than for show.

The holidays were drawing nearer; not fast enough for me. I missed my boys so much by now, it was a constant ache. I was so worried that they wouldn't like the house and never want to come back. Thanksgiving was a sad and lonely affair, just the two of us, and dear old Sandy. I put out the Thanksgiving decorations but there was no joy in the sight.

I had been planning to put on a big lunch and open the big doors and invite everybody in the neighbourhood in, like my own little street party. It was just the sort of thing that I used to do – organise events around food – but I suddenly lost all confidence in my ability to be with people. I kept the big doors shut and tried to avoid going out.

When we did go out we would explore little local places, and were constantly inspired by the age and beauty of the place where we were living.

We decided one day to find our way to the little hill town we could see across the valley from our house. It turned out to have a rather elegant name: *Fontana Liri Superiore* (as opposed to *Fontana Liri Inferiore* on the valley floor). I loved looking at the houses hewn from the cliffside, the tiny winding streets created centuries before cars were invented.

BLOG POST: FONTANA LIRI SUPERIORE WINE FESTIVAL (CANCELLED DUE TO RAIN)

The weather forecast was not promising, I'll admit. After weeks of dazzling sunshine and breath-snatching heat, it was bound to rain. Anything scheduled annually for October 27th & 28th is going to be chancy; I'm sure they've been rained off before.

But these sorts of festivals take time, coordination, energy, raw ingredients, baking, marquee erection skills, brochure design, courtesy bus hire, and possibly a low-key police presence to ensure safe and sensible parking. It is a tragedy in miniature when it gets rained off.

I was rather looking forward to this festival. We had visited the tiny town before, coiling cautiously up the snake-like ascent to the hilltop, parking dubiously, and wandering its doll-like streets, admiring its full-sized and breath-taking views.

We had been given a three-fold glossy colour brochure about the festival in the local hardware store, and the man in the hardware store mimed for us a delightful evening of wine, food, and, well, wine again. The courtesy bus ensured that visitors to the festival who might be concerned about drink-driving could safety arrive and depart without getting behind the wheel.

The brochure made great reading. Thirty venues were listed as vying for our attention, with such offerings as small gnocchi in scampi cream, crêpes, tortillas, chestnuts, polenta, spiralled potato crisps, tortiglioni carbonara, grilled pancetta with truffles, paella, and (with a nod to the Americans) hot dogs with ketchup. Fried pizza was in evidence, as it was in Colli, and fried fish; wine was scheduled to be in evidence everywhere.

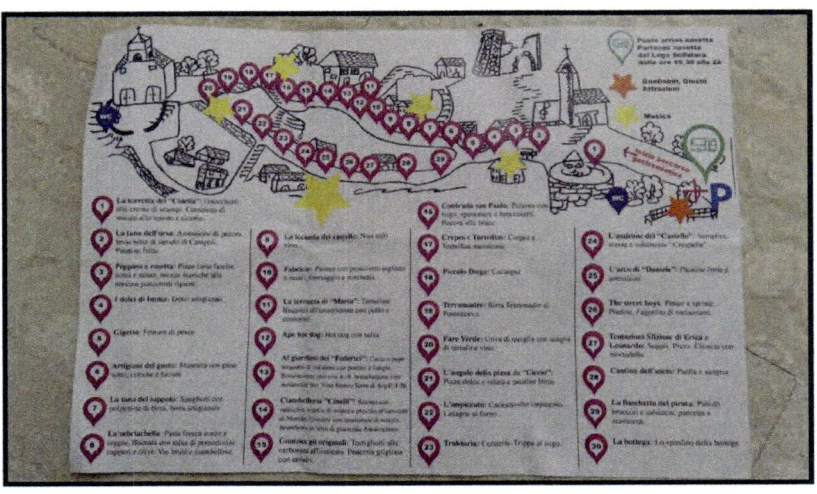

The festival was on a Saturday night and from noon onwards on the Sunday. We were at a mandolin concert on Saturday night so chose to visit on Sunday at lunchtime. Saturday night was a bit blowy and rainy. Sunday morning was blowy enough to merit closing all of the dark green wooden exterior shutters, and although the temperature gauge still read a balmy 21C it was wildy wet and windy by the time we left. We were hoping to be on the doorstep dead on noon, having had a light breakfast, and anticipating a glorious lunchtime.

I had one of those heart/head battles on the approach to the town. My heart desperately wished that the brave little town would, against all odds, hunker down and open the festival, taping, gluing, and nailing everything down that could conceivably blow away, and put a brave face on it all. But my head told me that it was very unlikely that there would be so much as a panini wrapper to be had in the town square; food tastes better out of doors, but rainy street food is not many people's idea of a good time.

Sure enough, we arrived in the square only to find a few forlorn, parked cars, wall papered with damp leaves, and a local mongrel dog supervising proceedings. My positive heart told me that everything was taking place higher up the hill, safely protected from the elements by the narrowness of the streets, and the height of the buildings. My negative head told me that absolutely *nothing of any interest was going on at all, anywhere.*

A dapper and soulful-looking gentleman ambled by, trying not to look too defeated by his umbrella, which was determined to turn itself inside out in the high wind. He confirmed that the festival had been cancelled, and he sorrowfully mimed rain. I wondered if he had left an exhausted wife at home, in her kitchen, wondering what on earth to do with eighty uneaten pizza bases and a mega-vat of pasta sauce.

There were strands of police tape pointlessly flapping about, a few metal curb barriers protecting nothing at all, and the street dog, eyeing up our car with the fervour of a Customs and Excise inspector. I am extremely fond of this tiny town, for no apparent reason apart from its charm, its minuteness, and its determination to hang onto the cliff on which it is perched, for as long as possible. I wished so many good things for this, its special festival day, but my wishes weren't strong enough, or my prayers were not heard; it was well and truly rained off.

People lived so close to one another. They could manage it; why couldn't I? I wished I could be a different person, a person with tolerance for other people's flaws, and idiosyncrasies, and noise. I tried to play my flute, something which used to give me joy. It felt wrong somehow, making my particular sort of noise and thinking that it was better than anyone else's noise. Why should my neighbours have to put up with that?

I began to feel so lost. What was I doing here?

One of the main reasons why we moved to Italy was for health reasons. Peter's arthritis and my asthma would benefit from the hot dry conditions. But now that we were here we were suffering from health problems of a different sort. The stone floors were killing me – really hurting my feet and legs – and Peter struggled to get to the top of the stairs, so much so that we had a chair for him on the half landing so he could rest on the way up.

I couldn't manage the language – didn't even try anymore. We had little translation stickers all over the house to help me with vocabulary, but suddenly the whole of a country's language seemed too overwhelming to me, and I somehow managed to get by with only a small handful of phrases that I'd picked up in the first few weeks.

I was dying to see my boys, but so fearful about what they would think of the house. I couldn't find the Christmas decorations. We couldn't find anyone who sold fresh cut Christmas trees. Christmas had always been a big event in our house, when the boys were small, but now I didn't seem to be able to go about it anymore. We were in a country so famously steeped in faith. Christmas just meant something very different over here.

I finally found one small box of decorations, and we splashed out and bought a fresh, live, potted tree, which would be a feature on our terrace throughout the year.

My attitude had changed so much. I just seemed to have a big hole inside. I couldn't remember how to be a parent.

Christmas

We finally got up the nerve to try the central heating system. It smelled a bit at first, burning and oily, and it took some time for the warmth to reach to the far tops of the house. We supplemented the heating with smaller electrical heaters. The heating oil ran out so fast. So we started to economise. Wearing warmer clothing. Additional layers. Keeping shutters shut in rooms we weren't using. We got in more gas heaters, and a steady stream of bombolas. It was the stuff of movies: two old folks dressed in their warmest winter clothing, huddling around an electric heater, tucked up in one room of an otherwise boarded up house.

When a high wind arose at night while the shutters were open they would whip and slam and bang, tempting us with protection and then withdrawing the offer, swinging in uncontrollable delight. Once a storm flared up with incredible speed. Every shutter in the house had sprung into life, slamming and cavorting in the high wind, throwing buckets of rain through the open windows and across everything in its path.

We had been so much warmer in Wiltshire. Apart from that one fluke weekend of snow it had never gotten that cold again for the rest of the year. England is so much further north than Italy but the houses are designed for winter, so we had been much more comfortable. We were used to intemperate conditions, but didn't ever dream that we would be experiencing it again in Central Italy.

The smooth cool marble floors of summer turned against us, virtually overnight. I felt a perennial ache in my head and took to wearing a woollen headpiece in bed. We made log fires in the cavernous pink fireplace, which had a cheering glow, but were no match for the painful, stone-cold stone.

That's when the real glacial weather hit us.

There was snowfall on the far mountains. People began burning anything and everything in their fireplaces, and the thick, pungent heavy smoke would creep down the lane, up the ancient walls, and across the terrace, choking and greying the brightness of the light. We agreed to economise with the heating when it was just the two us and splash out by turning on the radiators on the mornings when Teresa came to clean. We were saving up to heat the house properly when the boys arrived.

I wore a full-length parka in the kitchen when I made supper, the very same kitchen which I had sweltered and nearly fainted in during the baking heat of early autumn. I couldn't believe it was the same house. Sometimes I would go outside to get warm. I just didn't recognise Italy anymore.

An enormous nativity scene appeared in the villa square, taking up two valuable parking spaces and forcing us to park further down the steep hill. It was delightful, very carefully thought out, and executed. It had sand, and palm trees, and actually looked like the person who made it had actually been to Bethlehem. I'm not sure what Rome was like at Christmas time but there were very few traces of decoration in Colli. One or two houses had modest paper or tinsel ornaments on their doors, but none of the elaborate light displays we were used to seeing in California, and London. I chose a simple front door ornament: a collection of three outsized metal Christmas bells. They hung from one of the elegant wrought iron door knockers. The boys were with us by this time – arriving from different airports – but the mood in the house lifted tangibly, and I began to feel that we might have a festive Christmas after all.

One day I noticed that the Christmas ornament on our front door was missing. In the bigger scheme of things this isn't a tragedy, but it made me feel grubby, knowing someone had made off with our little bit of festive cheer. Other houses in the lane had decorations out: flashing lights, funny Santas, revolving LED gobos, nothing very pricey, but someone had nicked a lovely metal set of Christmas bells off of our door, probably not knowing that it had come from a posh London shop, or that they had a special sentimental significance to me.

I decided not to take this lying down, and we put up a sign – in Italian – asking for them back. Jaka assured me that they would never come back, and bitterly told us about his first few weeks here, in which *all of his clean laundry was stolen*. One day he actually met the thief in the village, parading around in his stolen clothes. When he'd confronted him, the man had claimed they were his own, brazenly defying Jaka and virtually daring him to challenge his remarks.

One evening the doorknockers went, cracking loudly during our meal. When my husband opened the door, a shifty looking man was there – whom Peter deduced immediately was the thief himself – in the lane, with my bells, crumpled and matted, but still intact. He claimed to have found them, and wanted a reward. We were floored. The thief and my husband had a very curious bi-lingual argument, as my husband had little Italian, and the thief had no English. They spat retorts at each other, the thief rubbing his fingers together in the universal gesture for money, and my husband clutching the mangled ornament and waving the man off into the street. Three times the man came back and thumped heavily on our door knockers, and three times he was sent packing. I winced inwardly, mortified at having tried to keep everything festive and happy for my boys, and having this depressing little scene being played out right under their noses.

We had the bells, we paid no reward. The bells stayed in the house. I feared for the contents of our Christmas parcel post box, parked as it was outside the front door, and open to the elements.

By now it must have been apparent to our sons that all was not right in this corner of Arcadia. We reluctantly came clean one night, and filled them in on the struggles we were having. Whatever feelings they were harbouring about our choice to relocate to Italy, they never revealed them. They just listened, and reassured us that that they were happy to be with us for the holidays, and that all would be well.

Gift-giving at Christmas is something which I have always enjoyed, but the choice to be in Italy added a particularly challenging element to the activity, and resulted in our making five visits to the tiny village of Strangoligalli. I had elected to send Italian dry goods to our friends for Christmas this year, little favourite foodstuffs that we had come across in the local markets, which I had not yet seen in Britain. Nothing illicit, nothing illegal to send in the post, just simple tasty treats. I carefully wrapped each item in an Italian tea towel, and after we parcel wrapped them for security, we looked at the various ways to post items safely abroad.

We had already had some experience with the local Italian postal service, which usually involved dedicating an entire morning to using the service, and involved queuing for an indefinite period of time with a good book. We had actually attempted to post the parcels twice already, once from our local post office (which was closed that day) and once from a tiny post office high up on a hill, whose computers were down. We had been carrying these parcels around for days, and as the holidays loomed nearer, we decided on an alternative course of action.

We felt that for packages going abroad, a dedicated parcel service would be the answer, and we chose UPS. The website was in English, the system seemed fool-proof and idiot-proof, and I thought I had figured out precisely what to do when we set out one morning for the aforementioned Strangoligalli.

Strangoligalli, in Italian, translates as "strangle the chicken". Or "strangle the rooster" depending on who you believe. The town crest has a shield with an image of a poultry-type creature battling a fox-like creature. The accurate history of the town really depends on whether or not you believe everything you read on Wikipedia, but despite the eccentricities of the name, it happened to be the closest UPS pick-up point for us. Following the instructions on the UPS website we made our way to a bar in the village, which like many bars in many Italian villages, was the heart of the village and served many purposes, including the postal service.

In total we made five visits to the village – including driving through it after we left the little hilltop post office – and only once did we ever make it directly, without getting lost. The sat-nav promised us a twelve-minute journey. The longest attempt took forty minutes, and the shortest journey, finally, was the promised twelve. We saw some beautiful scenery on our journey, and met some delightful people. If these particular elements of a journey have value -people and scenery - then they were very successful journeys. If the value of a journey to the post office lies in its brevity, then our journeys failed miserably.

When we first arrived in the town, we were amused to find that the bar we were destined for was in the centre of the town, on the corner of a busy crossroads, but virtually inaccessible due to the lack of parking. There were few road markings, and some very creative attempts at parking. Elderly men and dogs wandered about, criss-crossing the street, the men jovially chatting and laughing with each other and the dogs sniffing and rootling about for scraps of food.

The bar was a truly multi-purpose Italian style bar: long, L-shaped, and open-plan, with a variety of activities going on inside. Outside was a canvas covered terrace, with lightweight aluminium seating, ash trays, serviette holders, coasters, and everything suitable for socializing. Indoors there was a pinball arcade in one corner, a dining area, the bar itself, a long glass-topped pastry display case, and a large-screen television, which on this particular occasion was loudly airing clips of a speech by the Pope.

We went to the section of the bar where the coffee cups and espresso maker were housed, and waved our parcels at the woman behind the counter. We ordered two espressos and some delicious-looking pastries, as she took the parcels across to the till. To be honest I'm still not entirely sure what we did wrong, but I think it had something to do with the fact that we were supposed to print off some sort of label, or fill out some sort of form online, *before* going to the drop-off point. We had not done this, and the system began to break down. Clearly my research into *How to Post a Parcel in Italy* was nowhere near extensive enough.

The woman took out her personal laptop and began to investigate. Italian was spoken. She tried to explain our error to us, but the language barrier was too much for her, so she asked a customer, in rapid Italian, to go find *The Man in The Village Who Spoke English*. There seemed to be only one.

He soon appeared, slightly flushed but pleased to be asked to assist. Quite a lot of Italian was spoken this time, with contributions made by other people on both sides of the bar countertop. I think perhaps we had arrived on the wrong day, or perhaps the postman had already collected parcels for the day, or maybe it was a bank holiday, it was rather difficult to tell, but he eventually announced to us that *forms needed to be filled out* before anything could happen next.

The woman behind the bar, in true Italian fashion, went out of her way to help us. She offered to fill out the forms for us, online, using her personal computer.

We were charmed by this suggestion, and gratefully acquiesced. I glanced around the bar – it was a quiet time of the morning – and we settled down in chairs with our drinks and our pastries, watching the Pope blessing everyone with benevolence.

Almost immediately we were on our feet again. She needed information from us: phone numbers, addresses, emails, ours and theirs, value of contents, insurance, the lot. She ploughed through the form, with no outward signs of annoyance, but I still felt a bit of an idiot having so completely botched the simple task of preparing a parcel to post. For some of our friends, we had multiple addresses, phone numbers, and emails. We hissed to each other quickly:

"Is that Mandy's work number?"

"She works from home."

"I know, but only part time. Is this her old or her new work number?"

"Use her home number."

"Which one?"

"Is Estelle's email Yahoo or gmail?"

"I'm not sure, use both."

"There's not room on the form. Use ours."

"Which drop off point in Greenwich is closest to Peter & Illona?"

"I'm not sure; what's their postcode?"

"I can't remember; my diary is on my desk."

The bar was beginning to fill up; people were beginning to stare. The woman at the till, pure grace under pressure, was clearly beginning to regret her decision to help us. Finally, with a small Italianate flourish, she looked up from her tablet and said, through her interpreter, that she would finish the work overnight and have everything ready for tomorrow.

Everyone in the bar looked relieved, and in a flurry of *grazie milles* we abandoned the bar, diving into our car and reversing cautiously into the maze of cars, dogs, and men filling the street behind us.

Our third visit to Strangoligalli took even longer than the previous two, having foolishly elected to find our way without the sat-nav. This was the forty-minute version, and the annoyance of attempting the trip unaided make us irritable, adding to our frustration at not having succeeded in posting the items well and truly, on our first visit.

We arrived in a black mood.

As we entered the village, preparing to hunt for parking, a large funeral cortège crept solemnly down the middle of the street. Mourners processed on foot, as was the custom, and all activity in the hamlet came to a standstill. Obviously we were in no way part of this ceremony – we only wanted to park for a moment – but the sheer pressure to show respect halted us in our tracks, and we waited, fuming, as the stylish and shiny hearse slid past us, performing an elegant u-turn, and disappearing off down a tiny lane, taking its black cape of pedestrian mourners with it.

Once inside the bar, things got worse. She was not there. Another woman, who we did not recognise, was behind the bar. We mimed a bit, along the lines of *Englese*, and *parcels*, and *UPS*. She realized what we were there for and went to the till, miming things that we didn't understand and saying *domane*, tomorrow.

Visit number four was cautious and studious, following every twist and turn on the sat-nav, and hoping against hope that this would be the final, successful postal-related visit to Strangoligalli. We found a parking space, and our new friend was again behind the bar. We smiled, grazied, ordered even more espressos, and even more pastries. She explained that she had done all the work, everything was ready to go, but they hadn't gone yet because the post office wasn't open on a Monday. We forced a smile, paid in cash, drank our drinks, watched the footie on the big screen, and drove off happily into the morning sunshine, saying goodbye forever to Strangoligalli and its inhabitants.

Once back home, I had a nagging feeling that all was not right. We had no documentation about our deliveries. All of the work had been done on her personal laptop, we had paid in cash, we had no receipt. There was absolutely no evidence of these transactions, and no way of tracking them should they go astray. I couldn't believe it. This was a cock-up of epic proportions. I began to mentally tally the cost of the presents, the parcel wrap, the pastries, the espressos, the petrol, and the UPS postal charges, and my blood pressure went through the roof.

We had to pay another visit to Strangoligalli.

Fifth time lucky: we found parking, the sun was shining, the bar was gleaming, and our parcels were gone. Apparently we were no longer part of the equation. Once the parcels had left their drop-off point, the relationship was purely between the UPS and the recipients; they would be the ones to be notified about delivery times and addresses, and we were no longer of any use, or importance, to this transaction.

As we made our way carefully down the winding lanes beyond the village, we cleared our minds of any sort of sentimentality regarding our last visit to Strangoligalli. Because it might not be our last. Who knew what the future might bring? It was a pleasant little town, in a rural picture-postcard sort of way, and I wouldn't have been opposed to another nostalgic drink and a bun in the bar someday.

By Christmas Day we managed to get all four of us – and the dog – and the tree, and (most of) the presents, and (most of) the decorations, altogether in the same room at the same time. Things from abroad had gone astray in the post. Things we had posted through UPS had gone astray. I was determined to sit and enjoy what I had with me there in the room: my warm and loving family, together again at last.

The more I relished having my boys with us again, the more I could feel my heart bracing itself for their departure. I know, I know, be in the moment, savour *the now*, that's the received wisdom regarding situations like this. But I do suffer from the most poignant sense of *anticipated loss*. Always have, my entire life. And I never believe that I will survive loss. So this Christmas was like Victorian mourning stationery, elaborately composed, but black-bordered.

JOURNAL ENTRY

I was morosely coiling LED tree lights around my wrist and elbow, when suddenly I heard, outside, singing, and the soft shuffle of feet in the lane. Happy to have an excuse to stop coiling, I opened the window and looked out into the lane. A large procession was moving solemnly, and gracefully, down the tiny street, with the baby Jesus in a small silk-lined box, carried high up on poles, on the shoulders of six men. The priest was now intoning gently in Latin, and it was an utterly enchanting and unexpected moment. I watched the congregation all the way down the street until they were out of sight; a few whisps of Angels We Have Heard on High floated back at me as they disappeared from view. I actually felt quite blessed and comforted by this small and poignant scene.

New Year's Eve was uneventful, but the new year itself was ushered in with a small earthquake- more of a nudge really- but it was enough to awaken my Californian Earthquake Prevention Instincts, and I was up and under the doorframe like a shot. It was a very small earthquake really, and I felt a bit of a noodle standing there all by myself in the brace position. My husband stared mildly at me from the sofa; the dog snored quietly. I did have a fleeting image of what a more severe earthquake might be like, and then tried to block the image from my mind. Basically it involved getting my elderly husband, my elderly dog, and myself, under a door frame, in a swaying palazzo, very quickly; the outlook was not good.

Honeymoon Over

I just wanted to go home. I'd been feeling it for some time. And then thinking it for some time. But the decision to speak out loud about it took some time.

In the way that caffeine wears off and leaves you feeling dull and listless, my icy, stone-floored life was becoming unbearable. We were surrounded by beauty but not a part of it. I stopped trying to communicate with people. Hated going outside in case I met someone. Just didn't have the strength to conjure up my few feeble words of Italian to ask people how they were, or ask for things in shops.

I had made a little breakfast bar for us outside the bedroom on the first floor, and kept the makings for coffee in the bedroom, so I could just crawl out of bed in the mornings, cross to the coffee maker, and then retreat to the bed with two steaming mugs, hoping not to have to leave the bed for the rest of the day. But of course we did. We'd have our coffee, and something would drive us to get up, and out of the bedroom, and into Winter Italy.

I don't recall a single, momentous moment when we discussed moving back. You'd think there would've been a showdown of some sort but no, sometimes the biggest decisions in life are not necessarily framed in fireworks and fanfares. We were too cold and tired to have Big Moments.

We did have sporadic conversations about moving to another house in the same area, but we couldn't possibly imagine how we were going to sell this one, with all of its inherent problems. We didn't want to sell it to some unsuspecting foreigner. We figured that a savvy Italian would snap it up and make it magical for two, maybe three months out of the year. And besides, the call of home and family was too loud, to shrill, to be ignored.

I just wanted out.

I thought about all of the effort we had put into getting here. Two van loads of personal belongings, Tom and Tim and their dramas, our crazy mad trek across Western Europe in a stick-shift. All of the faffing about back in Britain trying to store the remainder of our stuff.

I thought about the boys. One was up in Liverpool. The other was down in Cardiff. We still had our cottage, piggy-in-the-middle in North Wales, no doubt snowed-in at the moment. Where would we go? Pretty much anywhere we went back to would mean travelling for somebody. But at least we would be home.

We finally agreed on a plan. It wasn't the sort of plan I usually like to make because it was very open-ended and sketchy around the edges, but it seemed to make sense. We were going to pack up as many essentials as we could in the car, put dear old Sandy somewhere comfortable on the back seat, and drive back home in order to find somewhere to live. And then we would extricate ourselves from Italy.

Money was really tight by this time. But we did it. We arrived back in Britain. I was in some sort of strange limbo, shell-shocked with the cold, and the stress, and the parental ache. But being that low can be liberating. I no longer had the energy to plan anything, to try to control or determine my own life. I just went with whatever was on offer. Very unlike me. But after all we had been through, I couldn't remain the same old me. Our journey to Britain this time had a completely different feel to it. We didn't pre-book anywhere. We would just stop when we felt like it, walk into some hotel or another, book a room on the spot. The only arrangements we'd actually pre-planned failed to materialise. Peter had a friend in Geneva, and we stopped by to say hello, hoping perhaps for a bed for the night. But she was a theatre producer, on the eve of a production, and her house was full of technicians, working late into the night. She gave us late afternoon tea, but apologised as she had no more room for unexpected guests. We were out on the road again.

I was trying not to panic, but we were at that point about to head into the French Alps, at sundown, with snow beginning to fall. Yet still we ploughed on, and just as the snow was getting really heavy we stumbled upon a tiny hamlet, picture postcard perfect, with the most delightful little Swiss chalet in the middle of it. We peered through the snow-dipped windows at a warm, jovial scene inside. As luck would have it, they had space for us, and our sleepy dog. This was perhaps one of the most enchanting rooms of our lives, this little chalet room, enchanting because we hadn't planned it, and because its warm red bedding, pine interiors, soft bedding and snow drifts outside the windows, were in such start contrast to the life we had left behind.

I flexed my parenting muscles, found them weak and flaccid. Glyn was happily ensconced in uni, had found a circle of friends and was living the undergrad lifestyle. Visiting him was one of our first stops back in the U.K. Dylan was less happy, having separated amicably from his girlfriend and found a room in a house from which he commuted daily to a teaching support job in a local sixth form college. We began to nudge towards moving to the Liverpool or Manchester area to help support Dylan.

We drove around England looking for somewhere to live. In the car I had packed our clothes, a folding catering table, two folding camping chairs, the dog bed, a kettle, some air mattresses, and the Thanksgiving table decorations (just in case we never went back to Italy, ever, and I had to leave all my personal belongings behind).

We so nearly settled in Hereford, a lovely, low-key county which we adored. It was equidistant between the two boys, but it meant that one or another of them would always have some travelling to do whenever we got together. Dylan, in the meantime, had been job hunting, trying to get himself out of a sort of rut he'd fallen into. Dylan applied for, and got, his dream job. He was hired to work at Old Trafford in Manchester, as a Disability Sport Cricket Coach. Dylan's life was devoted to cricket, and his coaching skills were fantastic. He was perfectly placed. We decided that we would find a rental property there for the three of us – and Sandy – to get us all back on our feet again

It would be a House of Healing.

I had begun to get really stressed about neighbours. I was so afraid of landing in a place with hidden flaws. We came across a lovely little 1930s double-fronted house in Sale, and when we drove by to check out the neighbourhood I couldn't bear to view it, because although it was in a pretty little tree-lined street of similar houses, the potential for disruption by other people was very high. Peter calmed me down, gave me some perspective.

We drove around the town, getting a feel for the place. It was quite surreal after life in Lazio. There was an ice-skating rink, a bowling alley, a McDonalds, several pizza take-aways. It felt soft and welcoming. Very suburban. Green and lush with beautiful parks. Comfortable. I insisted on going back to see the neighbourhood where that nice house was, at night, to see if it was noisy.

We drove down the well-manicured little street, looking at the houses and their quiet, considerate occupants, peacefully going about making their suppers, and boiling their kettles, and watching their BBC telly programmes. It was very quiet. Cars were parked neatly in their own driveways. The lawns were tidy and maintained. One or two dog walkers were about, with happy, smiling dogs.

I finally agreed to view the house and of course it was amazing. It was the antidote to Italy. It was carpeted, double glazed, bright and fresh, red brick and wood shingle, with a pocket kerchief garden for the dog, a gas fire you turned on with a remote control, a Jacuzzi bath, masses of space, bedroom for us, and Dylan, and Glyn, and guests. We leased it immediately. No questions asked.

Our flight was over. The eagles had landed. We were home.

To this day I couldn't possibly tell you why we moved to Italy. I thought it was to reinvent ourselves. What was wrong our old selves?

It was much, much more than a sort of March Hare Madness, much bigger than a seven-year itch. Not just about a cold house.

If I really had to define it I think I could say that I was testing my boundaries. I needed to find out how big I was inside. I needed to discover just how large the world really was, and although I'm not the sort of person to take a year out and globe trot, by living in a foreign country, it sort of answered those questions in miniature.

Perhaps I felt rejected by my children. What a silly thing to be feeling. They were doing what they were supposed to be doing: growing up, branching out, flying high. We let them do that. And we were left behind.

Perhaps we were defying our own mortality. By reinventing ourselves perhaps we were trying to extend our lives somehow, like an epilogue.

We made a few more trips to Italy after that, tying up loose ends. We had a glorious time. We revisited tourist Italy and reclaimed the joy we used to have. We floated in the salty sea at Vasto, the water as warm as the air. We dined al fresco in Sperlogna. We swam – pale as cod – next to impossibly bronzed Italians. It was a different country from the marble-edged life in Colli.

I now know how big – and small – I am. I know where I fit on the planet. Maybe I could have discovered that without moving to – and back from – Italy. Doesn't matter. The message is there.

Peter once said that he remembers vividly, as a child, looking down at his own little bedroom-slippered feet, and realised in that moment who he was, his sense of self, his uniqueness. Well, I'm now sixty-one, but at least I can look at my own two feet and have the recognition of knowing precisely who I am. Took a while, but I got there in the end.

Appendix I

MORE BLOG POSTS FROM ITALY FOOD TRAVELLER

IN DEFENCE OF MINESTRONE

Think about it: when you visualize the word minestrone, are you picturing something out of a tin, rather mushy and beige, thickened with excessive amounts of corn starch, laced with MSG, and including tiny cubes of unidentifiable vegetables? I used to loathe minestrone. It used to frequently be the vegetarian option on hospital dietary menus, served up religiously in school canteens, found tinned in mini marts which were open all hours. There always seemed to be several tins of minestrone on the shelves, even when the stocks of chicken noodle were running low. I assume, because nobody ever bought them.

I used to find it a really uninteresting mealtime option;

what was the point of choosing minestrone, in all of its vegetable blandness, when something else involving beef, pork, or lamb weighed in, with the promise of more flavour, more chunkiness, more hunger-satisfying munchiness?

My husband confirms that when he was a lad back in 1940's and 50's post-war, food-rationed Britain, minestrone was a culinary crime against humanity.

I made homemade minestrone for lunch the other day, and he looked positively betrayed. To be fair, when he asked what was for lunch, and I said minestrone, his childhood soup-related nightmares came back to haunt him.

What he couldn't have known was that I was down in the kitchen, rootling through the fridge/freezer, and extracting the most glorious, colourful, nutrition-packed and vibrant collection of ingredients for The Mother of All Minestrones. It read like a Who's Who of Vegetables from Mr MacGregor's Garden:

*Onion *Garlic *Celery *Carrot *Tomato
*Courgette *Peas *Green Beans *Spinach
*Mushrooms *Cannellini Beans

Then I started adding The Fun Stuff:

*Soup Pasta *Chicken stock *Grated Parmesan
*Pancetta lardons *Two heaped spoonfuls of Pesto
*Fresh basil, torn by hand *A dash of cayenne

*A swirl of extra virgin olive oil to finish
*Crusty bread on the side

To be fair, it was gilding the lily a bit, adding olive oil and pesto and basil and cheese, but I couldn't help myself: I was in some sort of culinary-induced trance whereby I ransacked the cupboards, hunting for even more and more delicious ingredients to fling into the soup kettle.

I softened the harder, root vegetables first, in olive oil and pancetta. After about ten minutes I added the more tender vegetables, the stock, and the soup pasta, simmering gently for about ten minutes, before finishing off the soup with the pesto, basil and cayenne. I put grated cheese in the bottom of each bowl and ladled the hot soup over the cheese. Crusty bread on the side needs no explanation; human beings are hard-wired to know what to do with crusty bread.

I actually am not too keen on the Italian habit of including pasta and beans together in the same soup as it seems too heavy, but the weather has been so cold recently, and our beautiful new house is so marble-y and so cold, that piling on the complex carbohydrates seems just the thing to keep us warm, and healthy, and nourished.

Because that's the fun of minestrone: whether you prepare it as a destination recipe, or an all-spare-parts Sunday night leftovers type of thing, it can really always be delightful. Which is why it is so commonly seen on menus. But maybe not always so delightful.

Please always try to use fresh, or freshly frozen ingredients. They look better, they taste better, they feel better on the tongue. Leftover stewing vegetables just don't hack it, and all of the nutrition will have been cooked out of them in the first half hour.

Looking over my recent posts, I seemed to have become some sort of champion of Popular Italian Food. I've defended Spaghetti Bolognese, Neapolitan Ice Cream, and now this. They can be fabulous foodstuffs, which is why they are popular, and why companies try to mass-produce them, but so much gets lost in translation when they are not made well.

Honestly, this is just a thick vegetable soup. The veggie-hating inner child in you may be resisting this soup with every fibre in your being, but I encourage you to try it, just once, homemade, and let your imagination run away with you. You may, oh so easily, become a convert too.

NEAPOLITAN ICE CREAM

Neapolitan ice cream is misunderstood, in my opinion. When I was a kid, Neapolitan was treated like the United Nations of Desserts, a democratic division of flavours to suit all palates, resolving conflicts at the dinner table, and uniting warring siblings in front of the fridge door, umming and ahhing about who-gets-what for dessert.

My father tried, once, to test the maturity of my sisters and me, by buying a large tub of Neapolitan ice cream and placing it in the freezer, and inviting us to have some. Given no instructions or parameters for this dessert, my sisters and I did what any normal, sensible, California kid of our generation would do: we dug out all of the chocolate layer, about half of the vanilla, and none of the strawberry. I do suspect we were being set up to fail.

My father then imposed sanctions on the freezer compartment. No one was allowed to have any Neapolitan ice cream unless they cut an even swathe across all three flavours with the ice cream scoop. Any uneven distribution of the chocolate end of things would result in immediate banishment from the ice cream department.

I'm not sure that we ever bought another tub of Neapolitan after that incident; we couldn't see the point. In fact, up until about a month ago I don't think I have ever purchased Neapolitan in a shop ever, or even ordered it in a restaurant. That was a pretty powerful experiment my father did, way back then.

But as you can see from the above picture, I did purchase some Neapolitan ice cream, as an adult, of my own free will, in a Co-op in Wiltshire. I think the sheer excitement of the pending move to Italy just got into my bones and made me a little bit crazy, and I suddenly started branching out and doing unusual things. It tasted pretty much as I remembered it from my childhood, but I was somewhat bolstered by the knowledge that my youngest son actually likes strawberry ice cream, and my husband is a vanilla kind of guy, and between my eldest son and myself we can battle over the chocolate together.

But what I really must tell you about Neapolitan is that it used to be a high-status dessert in America, and it was brought across from Italy by immigrant Italian chefs who were highly respected, and because so many of them came from Naples and the south of the country, the ice cream was dubbed Neapolitan. These skilled chefs were expert at creating lovely desserts, specifically ice cream desserts, and the three colour look of Neapolitan was supposed to emulate the Italian flag.

"Wait a minute!" I hear you exclaim, "the Italian flag is not brown, white and pink", and of course you'd be right. But the Italian flag is red, white and green, and the original Neapolitan ice cream was made with strawberry, vanilla, and pistachio. This would be reminiscent of Italian spumoni, with candied fruit and nuts in it. Apparently, the pistachio element wasn't as popular in the U.S., so chocolate was substituted, resulting in the culinary battle hosted in my childhood home, as recounted above.

Now I'll be honest and tell you that I began this blog post in England, before we moved house, but I am finishing it here, in Italy, with new, updated information. I have just recently had a four-flavour ice cream tub. Unbelievably cool. It consisted of vanilla, chocolate, chocolate chip, and walnut. The chocolate was a dark rich colour, the vanilla was surprisingly white, not creamy, the chocolate chip was chippy, and the walnut had a golden, caramel-sort of hue, quite complementary to the other flavours.

But what I think is the most important piece of information I have to impart to you, is that I, at the ripe old age of 58, scooped my ice cream democratically, and maturely, across all four flavours, just as my father would have wished. I like to feel that he looked down at me, smiling approvingly, as I made such a grown-up display of restraint, made even more difficult by the fact that the walnut flavour wasn't, well, really as delicious as its amber colour led us to believe.

So, the next time you see Neapolitan ice cream in a shop, or on a menu, show some respect. Think of the allusion to the flag, and the bravely skilled Neapolitan chefs who embarked on a journey to a brave new world, bringing their ice cream and dessert skills with them. Dare yourself to take a spoonful of all three at the same time, and let the flavours roll around and mingle on your tongue, as they were designed to do.

History makes food taste better. Dive in, and enjoy.

SPAG BOL

This is a really ugly nickname for a really lovely dish. I think it deserves better. This is the name for a cheap-eats, corner-cutting concoction that often comes out at fund-raisers, sporting events, and university knees-ups. Yes it can be inexpensive to make – but it doesn't have to be – and yes you can make it in a jiffy with a jar  of ready-made sauce and a packet of dried pasta, but it doesn't have to be that either.

I have just finished a little obsessive research session about proper spaghetti bolognese, and I've decided that (1) it is versatile (2) it is personal (3) it has regional variations and (4) it really isn't, in my opinion, worth coming to blows over the definitive recipe for spaghetti bolognese, because Italian food is by its very nature regional, and regional variations on spaghetti bolognese aren't wrong, they're just, well, regional.

I mean, think about it: pasta and meat sauce. It could've been invented anywhere, a million times over, by people who have never been to Bologna, and don't even know where it is. So it's not necessarily a regional recipe. And if you're cooking seasonally, then you've got to have seasonal variations on your spaghetti bolognese, so really, I feel that it is really important to find the recipe of your dreams that suits your tastes, budget, and regional variation. Call it a ragu. Many people do. Or even ragout.

I tried to find the difference between bolognese and ragu. Have you ever had the annoying experience of looking up a question online, and then having a writer promise to give you an answer to your question, and then waffle on a bit and then end the article without actually answering the question? Well, this was my experience of the ragu/bolognese question. People talked about white wine and red wine, and the ratio between tomato and meat, and Northern and Southern variations, and some people threw in terms like Neapolitan and marinara just to confuse. As far as I can tell, bolognese is a type of ragu.

During my little fact-finding mission I discovered many different recipes for ragu, which included the following ingredients: lemon juice, lemon zest, chicken livers, sausage meat, pancetta, pork, veal or beef mince, cream, white wine, red wine, red onions, white onions, yellow onions, condensed tomato paste, passata, fresh tomatoes, fresh cultivated mushrooms, dried porcini mushrooms, herbs, (and also absolutely no herbs don't even think about adding herbs), cheese, no cheese, and these are just ingredients for the sauce. I also read once, and only once, the suggestion that you should use garlic or onion, in your sauces, but never both at the same time. (This I read about in a cookery book in the bedroom of a rather splendid hotel. I believe alcohol may have been present at the time so perhaps I have got this wrong because I have never read it before or since but I do think it's an interesting idea...)

The recommended pasta shapes have included pappardelle, tagliatelle, fettucine, and lasagne noodles, green or white, but the one thing that everyone seems to agree on is never use spaghetti noodles for spaghetti bolognese because the sauce just slips off the noodle and ends up on your shirt. That's ironic, really, considering when you ask for spaghetti you are asking for the shape of noodle not the sauce, and what you should really be asking for is ragu or bolognese, hold the spaghetti.

Matchthepastatothesaucematchthepastatothesaucematchthepastatothesauce is the mantra.

I keep coming across the term "bronze die cut" pasta, which basically means that the noodle, when extracted, has more texture to it – for the sauce to cling to – and therefore you get more pasta in your mouth and less on your clothing. It is actually true, and I don't think it's a gimmick. After cooking a rich sauce for an hour or so, I'd like to ensure somehow that I actually get to eat it, and not wear it.

In my own kitchen, I vary my ragu depending on where I am and what is local, seasonal, and fresh. In winter, reconstituted dried porcini mushrooms add a lovely depth of flavour to the sauce, but in autumn fresh mushrooms look very inviting. A summer bolognese may have stacks of sweet peppers and fresh tomatoes instead of passata. Pancetta lardons are great in a bolognese made in Italy, but in the States the crispy bacon is full of flavour, and in Britain streaky bacon is the best substitute. In Italy, I've just come across little cartons of flavoured savoury cream, such as salmon, truffle, and porcini; a small carton of porcini cream swirled through as a finishing touch before serving is really heavenly.

There is one unfortunate element to the preparation, though. The longer you cook vegetables, the less nutritious they are. But one of the most important requirements for a good ragout is a long slow cook, and also that the vegetables are soffrito - slowly cooked - even before the meat is added. So, in terms of nutritional value, I'm not sure that spaghetti bolognese is going to be your star player. I think it's a trade-off with pure comfort value, and therefore the obligatory green salad on the side is going to be very important here, in terms of your five-a-day. (In a stew, by the way, as opposed to a ragu, if you use big chunky vegetables for the stewing process, it's a good idea to remove the pieces of stewing vegetable once they've served their purpose, and 'refresh' the stew with new vegetables towards the end of the cooking time. This gives the nutrition, colour, and texture you crave).

Seriously: develop a recipe for spaghetti bolognese and 'make it your own'. Make something so personal and unique to you that your friends will beg for the recipe and it will become a family heirloom passed down through generations. Your son's new wife will ask for the recipe, and attempt to make it, when you and your husband come to visit. And it won't be as good, according to your son, but then his new bride will find her own special recipe, and on it will go. I think what I'm saying is, don't be bullied into so-called 'authentic' or 'traditional' recipes unless it is really important to you to be authentic or traditional. Finding your own culinary voice is just as important, and ultimately more rewarding.

TAKING 'DIET' OUT OF THE MEDITERRANEAN DIET

We're in Lazio, halfway down the 'shin' of the Italian boot.

In terms of cuisine, cooks are thinking about reaching for olive oil, in the Southern style, rather than butter, more traditional up North.

We've been dining daily on a diet of grilled fish, chicken, and meat, with a slice of lemon to dress it. The salads are light and fresh, and without a hint of mayo or salad cream. We see Parmesan optional on the table, and the occasional ball of buffalo mozzarella, plus the local ewes' milk cheeses, and Pecorino Romana. Risotto is served plainly with grilled mushrooms, or seafood, but doesn't seem to have the handful of Parmesan and large dollop of butter which I usually use to finish off my dish at home. We had the most divine frittata yesterday: thinly sliced zucchini, sautéed, and bound together with the lightest of egg bases, nothing like the chunky wedges of potato-cheese-and-onion dishes which I make, a bit like high-cholesterol doorstops.

I love the fact that salt and pepper do not appear on the table. Trust chef.

How can this be called a 'diet'? I understand that the word 'diet' can mean (1) the foodstuffs used by a particular culture or population, in addition to (2) low calorie, healthy, weight-loss menus. I think the word 'diet' makes you feel like you are going to suffer, somehow, or do without. It implies that you must bring a calculator to the dinner table, and pine for things in the middle of the night, lying awake, glassy-eyed at 3 a.m., dreaming of a 'fridge raid. I think Mediterranean Lifestyle might be a bit more helpful and a little less stoical, and a lot easier to stick to for the long haul.

There have been fresh figs for breakfast each morning: giant soft green, nearly the size of tennis balls, and so tender, it seems you could cut them with a feather, before gently peeling them backwards and eating them without the need for cutlery. I was thinking of all the ways to play with theses figs in the kitchen: grilling, poaching, dotting with butter and stuffing with cheeses and drizzling with honey and spices. I asked in the kitchen if they ever grill their figs and they looked at me a bit oddly, and I did feel a bit foolish. When it's fig season, have figs. When you have a lot of figs, make jam. Life can actually be that uncomplicated, if you want it to be. Each morning different fruit appeared: golden plums, nectarines, pineapple, more figs. A wedge of melon appeared on an antipasti platter before the main course. Who says fruit must always come at the end? We drove past the market square one morning and were curious to see the huge market day lorry being unloaded. Enormous watermelons were piled precariously high in the early morning sunshine, and all sorts of interesting-looking crates and boxes were being brought out, a veritable toy store for me to play in when we have made the move, and put our suitcases away for good.

There was a wedding at the hotel. They host large functions here on a regular basis, so there was a confident, assured pace about the place as the preparations progressed. There are two grills in the kitchen, one on each floor, and these are used quite frequently during the week and for their big functions.

There was such charm about this wedding; I was entranced. Tables were laid out across the entire terrace – each with an exquisite view of the surrounding hills. Simple glass jars held simple floral arrangements, and the cream white and green colour scheme blended effortlessly into the scenery. There was nothing strident about this affair. Guests made their appearances, smiling and laughing, dressed comfortably for the summer heat. Children giggled and ran about. Nobody suffered in a too-tight rental suit; no one struggled with tight waistbands and tiny pointless hats. There was a live band with wedding classics, which from my bedroom window may not have been ideal, but I've no doubt that for the guests on the terrace, with champagne in hand and blessed with an amber sunset mellowed into a haze of food, and wine, and dancing, and romance.

We were offered the wedding starter course: a choice of either a mixed fish, or meats platter. The fish option was simple but elegant, a composed platter of calamari, oysters, mussels, scampi, very thinly sliced salmon, and a white flatfish I couldn't identify. It was all set off with a single slice of lemon and a leaf of radicchio. I'm sorry I didn't have my camera to take a picture for you; I didn't want to intrude on their party. I love the idea that, on a festive occasion, it doesn't mean you have to have food that isn't good for you. I think that somehow the British and American cultures have got this sort of mixed-up idea that treat food, and party food, has to be unhealthy food, that something can only be celebratory if it's got mayonnaise on it, is deep-fried, includes a crust on it, or has chips on the side.

Perhaps the Italians have such a great pride in their own regional cuisines – their incredibly ancient cuisines – that they haven't felt the need to adopt all of the rubbishy food trends lurching over here from America. It's encouraging. It's inspiring. It genuinely makes me feel like we're headed off in the right direction by moving here, opting for sunshine, fresh air and a slice of lemon, and leaving the Great British Breakfast behind.

VEROLI MARKET DAY

The Veroli street market is a gentle affair. Nobody heckles. You are not accosted by a florid-faced fruit stall holder, shoving three bunches of green bananas under your nose and bellowing "Get your bananas here, three for't price o' two!" using his outdoor voice to excess.

On a mild, sunny October morning I sauntered down the narrow street that is Veroli street market. At first we couldn't find it. The only online guidance I had was that it was in the centre of the town. But, as is true in many of these Italian hilltop towns, geography wins out, and the narrow streets at the bottom of the town become even more narrow higher up the hill, and if you can't read the warning signs in Italian, common sense will tell you that if you proceed any further you will pay the price of admission with one – or even two – smashed wing mirrors. The streets are so pretty near the top: breathtakingly tiny, geometrically and artfully decorated with multi-coloured cobblestones. If you're really lucky you may happen upon a camponile, or perhaps a monastery, at the top of these hills; sometimes you may find a vista point, or a terrace with benches. Sometimes you just find the other side, and a steep descent.

Having staggered to the top of the town in our rather large 4x4, and finding no sign of the market, we backed shamefully down again. My husband parked temporarily, and I made my way down the hill outside of the town walls, towards a promising collection of canvas umbrellas and jersey knit items dangling in the breeze. The entire market was situated down one particular main road, edged on one side by precariously perched homes, and fringed on the other side by glorious views out across the valley. One or two ambitious and wily stall holders had pitched camp inside the town walls, hoping to catch customers as they parked their cars, but for the most part the market ambled slowly down a gently sloping hill, tree-lined and paved, with a treacherously deep gutter slashed through the thoroughfare.

A woman with currant buns perched in solitude at the top of the hill; a jaunty display of boys' Italian football jerseys, and camouflage trousers was next, flapping in the breeze. After a small gap, the market continued in earnest. Huge stalls filled with kitchen equipment and linens gave way to children's shoes, play clothes, and virulent lingerie. A cool, refreshing block was given over exclusively to fresh vegetables, fruit, and a myriad of lettuce seedlings, destined for allotments and greenhouses all over the town. A stout, well-stocked stall had an incongruous selection: boiled sweets, thick chunks of salted fish, and an impressive collection of unmarked cheeses.

Traditionally, food tastes better out of doors. I have to say, I think pretty much anything you might consider buying on market day sells better out of doors. Plastic tubs and bowls, tureens, metal canteens, scrubbing brushes and brightly coloured dusters, all looked like much more fun to use when purchased from an outdoor stall. Washing up bowls which I would have passed by in a shop without batting an eyelid suddenly sprang to life and looked incredibly tempting: swimming pool blue, larger than life, endlessly cheerful. Slim jersey knit jumpers, when folded neatly and tucked away in a clothing store window, look sedate and sensible. But let them loose, on a plastic hanger in the Italianate breeze, and they dance joyfully, carefree, with a hi-viz handwritten label proudly announcing "10 Euros only"!

My husband appeared, triumphant, the proud owner of a second-hand whistling kettle, knocked down viciously from 20 Euros to a mere 8. Bartering and haggling make me shrivel shyly inside, so my husband took over the negotiations with all the ruthlessness of a City trader. I carried the bags.

We finally got down to business at a large deli-style stall, displaying large trays of shiny, brightly coloured dried fruit, fresh nuts, and nearly a dozen different types of green and black olives. Behind the stall was a truck crammed to the rooftop with meats and cheeses of all kinds, and slicing equipment. A kindly lady stall owner offered us samples of anything that caught our eye, and we left, laden down with kitchen foodie treasures to last us the whole week.

Soft blankets, bright white cotton sheets, table linens, shoes and toys, all were out on display in the warm sunlight with incredible confidence. Packing this lot up during a quickfire thunderstorm would have been a major operation, but the stall holders had the confidence to know that it wouldn't dare rain on Market Day, and they displayed accordingly, with panache.

I can't imagine how long it takes to unpack, and pack up, all of this merchandise, but it must be worth their while to visit Veroli every Tuesday to set up shop and trade for an entire day out-of-doors. There are markets scattered all over our part of Lazio, each no doubt with their particular style, flair, and personality. It's a social activity, a community commitment, a small slice of history each week, and it can just be good old-fashioned fun. I thank the stall holders of Veroli for their courage and their industriousness, and I wish them well. No doubt we'll be back. I think maybe I really need a washing up bowl...

A LETTER TO MY GREAT NIECE, TRAVELLING TO ROME

Dear Ella,

As you may be aware, I am incredibly geeky, and you are incredibly cool, so when I offered to advise you on your upcoming visit to Rome I think it was with the obvious proviso that this would be advice from a geek's point of view, and may be somewhat skewed in the direction of anxiety, awkwardness, and uncertainty. But somebody's gotta do it.

I know nothing about your circumstances, whether or not you are travelling solo, or with an army, who knows. This is just what I've picked up recently about travelling through Rome, and contributes nothing at all useful about sightseeing, or being a tourist in Rome, as those joys have yet to come, for me.

Shoes

Since you're travelling in July wear something cool, breathable, lightweight, but with good ,cushioned soles for lots of tramping on pavement. (See: I told you this would be sensible and geeky...) Those dainty flat-footed leather sandals with barely-there straps and a flourish of diamante aren't enough support, and your feet will ache. Also, if someone steps on your foot or worse, parks their suitcase on your foot, you will suffer, and possibly bleed. Getting blood out of diamante is a bitch. (I read the advice about closed-toe shoes in somebody else's blog and it hasn't happened to me, fingers crossed, but it could happen to anybody).

Also, every female in Italy seems to varnish their nails. Except me. Because I am a geek. (I'm too cheap to buy a pedicure, and when I tried to paint my nails myself, as a little kid, it drove me to distraction because I cannot seem to paint within the lines.) Sensible shoes keep my secret a secret. But if you are, as it were, bearing the foot-flesh in a cunning little shoe with dreamy detailing around the ankle, and all ten toes exposed, then by all means, paint away. People will notice, and admire.

Rail Travel

I love the Italian rail network. We just had the most delightful, cool, and comfortable journey yesterday, marred only by one thing. The train we were destined to catch was delayed by 90 minutes, but when an earlier one came along, to the same destination, we jumped on it with delight. It wasn't until we had nearly arrived in Rome that the ticket inspector caught up with us, and looked annoyed.

"Why are you on this train?" he demanded, in not-too-terrible English.

We stammered something about delayed trains and alternative trains and "windows of opportunity" but he was having none of it. Having lived in New York for many years, he had perfected the art of irate. Apparently, if you're on the Leonardo Express rail service from Rome Termini to the airport, and you miss your desired train, you do indeed have a 90-minute window of opportunity in which to catch a later train without buying another ticket. And on all other TrenItalia rail services you have a four-hour window. But you cannot take an earlier train than the one you have bought your ticket for, because their insurance cover for your journey doesn't kick-in until the train that you have bought a ticket for. We had to buy a completely new set of tickets, two minutes from our destination.

By the way, nearly every train in Italy seems to go into, or out of, Roma Termini. It's just a part of everybody's journey. That's probably why they have such a whacking great food court there. They don't appear to have food service on Italian trains, or at least they didn't on the ones we've been using, but there are often snack shops and cafés at the individual stations.

Asking For Help

There are people in the train terminal with official TrenItalia uniforms on, and there is an information desk at Rome Termini station. Be careful about just asking some guy with a nice face. We were stood standing by the big information screen trying to find our train platform, when a kindly looking grandfatherly gentleman came up to us and asked if we needed information about our journey. He had a nifty little low-slung leather wallet at his hip, which looked like an official ticket-inspector's bag, and he looked about Peter's age. He took us across to the ticket machine and looked up our train for us, and when Peter took the tickets out of the machine, he thanked the gentleman for his help. The guy held out his hand in expectation of money. Cash was tight for us, as we needed to find a bank as well, and this was really not an option. Peter refused, and the guy got a bit nasty-looking. We were firm and walked away but it was uncomfortable, and if he had been a bit younger and heftier, we would have really been worried. Also, if you take a taxi, only use taxis with the little white box on the roof because they are the legitimate ones. There will be a taxi rank at the airport, and the train station.

Safety

My first visit to Rome was scarred by a blogpost I read, about how much crime and theft there is in Rome, and how everybody is a pickpocket or worse. The waiters'll rip you off, the taxis will rip you off, the hotels will really rip you off. I was petrified. I practically held my breath the entire time we were passing through, and I clutched my handbag so close to my chest the entire time, I nearly suffocated. This is geek-based survival mode. We've been through about five times now, since reading that post, and I've decided that you're more likely to become a target if you exude terror and vulnerability, than if you adopt the air of savvy traveller, out on a lark.

Apparently, common-sense is the order of the day. I have none, unfortunately, so I needed to learn this by rote, but it does sink in after a while, and is a skill which can be taught. For example, you will be vulnerable while you are standing under the big sign with all of the platform listings, because you will be concentrating on a scramble of slowly-moving Italian place-names, trying to find out if anything even remotely pertains to you. Just develop a sixth sense for where your valuables are, and make sure you can feel your luggage touching you at all times, even if it is just your leg. I use a Healthy Back Bag, which allow me to sling it across one shoulder and have the internal pocket with my wallet in it facing towards me, pressed up against my stomach. Don't even think about putting anything in a back pocket, apart from possibly a really snotty used tissue, just for fun.

You may also be vulnerable getting on and off trains, and in transition at airports. Everybody is. Just act confident, like you know where you're going, and if you don't know where you're going, step out of the mainstream for a moment, park on a bench, and figure it out, instead of wandering about looking helpless and a little bit fragile.

I have found the most incredible grace and charm in the Italians I have met, and so when you are dealing with the right person in the right job I think you will find it will be a very pleasant experience.

Allow more time than you think you need. This is true everywhere you travel. Once we missed the last train of the night and had to, on spec, check into a hotel for the night. Luckily there is a very nice one called NH Collection hotel, just outside the Roma Termini, with a stellar breakfast spread, and right behind it is a Best Western. No need for taxis or faffing about; it's right next door. There were three of us travelling, and they made up a sofa bed in a Junior Suite for us which made a very comfortable double bedroom configuration.

When we missed the last train, and my anxiety levels were at their peak, we asked a female ticket inspector what to do and she directed us to go out of the train station (to the right, which is safer, not to the left) and we would find something, which of course we did.

If you are going to do the sights there is plenty of online information about Rome. We haven't done the city sights yet because we want the crowds and temperatures to go down first. I have read several times that there are dress codes for some attractions and sites, and this is essential to read up on. As an amateur people-watcher, I have my own likes and dislikes. I love watching elegantly-dressed travellers in airports and hotels, and have never ceased to be amazed by the number of people who think they can fit very large bodies into very tiny clothes and think they can manoeuvre into, and out of, public transportation, without things wiggling and going awol. Dressing for hot weather is an art form.

I'm going to stop now. Have a great trip!

With love,

Great-Aunt Marcie

THE PSYCHOLOGY OF PINK

A quick Google tells you everything you need to know about human beings and the colour pink. In branding, pink evokes femininity, happiness, playfulness, sweetness, love, health and romance. It's very girly. Barbie is at her best when dressed in pink. Research carried out in American prisons proved that the colour pink lowered blood pressure and had a calming effect on inmates, leading to a less volatile environment.

The fireplace in my new house is made of pink marble. Pink marble and pink granite. What a bold choice! This was a 17th c. Italian choice, at a time historically when

people had no access to MTV, digital cameras, and photography, and so expressed themselves through art, music, literature, and architecture. My house is in Lazio, a region of Italy which, without being described as unrefined, is most impressive due to its jagged landscapes, steep peaks and rough troughs. It lacks the water-softened gentleness of the river valleys, and the classical elegance of Rome itself. I'm not sure yet, but it's possible the winters here may be harsh. So what on Earth is a pink marble fireplace doing in Ciociaria?

Whoever chose this pink marble fireplace, five centuries ago, had a certain confidence of style and, I suspect, a generosity of pocket, to be able to place an order for such an extravagant creation. But attached to the fire surround, on either side, is a rather jarring note: an extremely sensible, narrow wooden bookcase, embedded into the marble. I think this was the husband's input. I imagine, perhaps an enormous battle raged, perhaps for weeks, about whether to splash out for a pink fireplace, or built-in wooden bookcases, with the poor architect or designer caught, piggy-in-the-middle, hunkering down until a decision was reached.

The compromise, between the self-styled pink-tinged chatelaine and her eminently sensible book-loving husband, was to choose the pinkest of pink Rosa Travertine tumbled pink marble from Verona and stick a small bookcase on the side.

"This is my house too!" he bellows. "I have to live here!"

"Try not to display, so obviously, my darling, your boorish country roots," she hisses malevolently, kicking marble tile samples across the floor and ringing the servants bell vehemently for an espresso.

But wait: what about pink? What does pink do to us? What about pink and romance, and sweet femininity, and the prisons in America? I doubt, upon reflection, that such an argument ever occurred in such a lovely room. Possibly it was a mutually book-loving couple with a shared love of entertaining who requested this confection.

The fact of the matter is, that 500 years later, I have purchased this house, and this fireplace, and it is down to me, the new owner, to responsibly maintain this fireplace, and incorporate its colour into my designs. My husband thinks it's a later addition, this bookcase, but if that's the case, then it doesn't make for as lovely a story.

Digressing slightly, I really would love to visit an Italian marble quarry someday. I can't imagine what a sheet rock wall of candy pink marble looks like. Does it pick up and reflect sunlight? It must make the entire area glow pinkly and girlishly. If you go to an Italian marble website like www.italymarble.com you will see the most astonishing array of brightly - and subtly - coloured marble. I wonder if people, when faced with such an impressive array of colours, go mad and choose shades that are perhaps slightly outside the bounds of architectural propriety, in the same way that a bathroom superstore inspires people to go OTT with kitchen and bathroom tiling.

I remember chatting with a stonemason who was building an extension for us, onto a stone cottage in North Wales. He showed me the wall he was building, and a pile of grey granite stones of various shapes and sizes. He pointed to the stones, and began to describe the subtlety of their shading. Some were pink grey, or blue grey, and dark as well as light grey. When somebody points it out to you, you can really see the difference. He was carefully orchestrating this wall to be a subtle harmony of all of these different tones of grey stone – no similar colours next to each other – and it was turning into a really beautiful piece of architectural work.

Well, this Welsh granite stone wall was really subtle, but the bouquet of marble shades on the Italian marble website is truly breath-taking. You can see the results in the astonishing and elegant palazzos, villas, and important buildings all over Italy. And here I've got my little pink patch of stone elegance to play with.

I started researching 17th century Italian design. The images online tended to polarize between massive noble palazzos in Florence, and chalk-white conical peasant cottages in Puglia. There were screeds of Tuscan farmhouses, cleverly, and not-so-cleverly, restored by the English. I had difficulty in finding just the right sort of image to suit my little country palazzo wing. (Apparently, if you decide to go house-hunting in Italy, if the building is a Palazzo with a capital "P" then it is the home of a royal family, and if it's a lower case "p" then it is a noble, but not royal, family).

Our new house is only one small slice of a larger Italian pie. The palazzo, within which it lies, is much larger, spreads all the way down the street, and incorporates the semi-detached village church (which used to be the private church for the family in the palazzo). There are patterns laid into the pavement in front of the house and in the square: designs in multi-coloured cobblestones of incredible charm.

But the pink; the incredibly pink fireplace. Where does this fit into the grander scheme of things? I look around the square, and the small street, and the house itself, and everything seems so solid, and sensible, a bit country but not in a country yokel sort of way. The quick glimpse I had of the church revealed gilt paint and high vaulted ceilings, and a very tender Madonna gazing softly across the sturdy oak pews. I saw no evidence, no warning, that once you had been through all the rooms in the house, worked your way up and up to the top floor room with the best view, that you would suddenly be confronted with a candy pink marble fireplace. It just comes at you, like a sudden stabbing flash of sunlight on a mirror.

If you've ever been inside an Italian villa, or palazzo,

or townhouse of any decent proportion you will begin to recognize re-occurring themes in the basic structure, such as vaulted ceilings in the lower rooms, wide hallways, large breeze-blessed tall windows, wrought iron balconies, rooms of good balanced proportions, cool marble and stone, and grace everywhere. We found this exquisite spiral staircase in an empty villa for sale. So so simple, so graceful.

I think the Italians, as a country, are in love with air. With space. With large boundaries. This love is reflected in the homes, palaces, parks, avenues, costumes, gestures, music and food of the nation.

As I wander through my new house and inspect small details that escaped my notice before, I see in my own home the love of air everywhere. Someone had a go at hand-painted friezes on the cupboard doors. I just love that. Someone was inspired enough to dig out the old watercolour set, or crimped set of oil paints, and actually sat patiently ornamenting the cupboards. Alcohol may have been involved, as the friezes (green boughs) go slightly skewwiff in places.

The staircase is elegant, and chunky, at the same time. The ceiling is impossibly high, and the intricate iron balustrades march firmly up the weighty granite stair treads. But suddenly, when you least expect it, the underside of the staircase curls girlishly in on itself, in a sort of architectural simper; it is just delightful. I love this house.

Of course there is another possible reason for the existence of a pink marble fireplace in my new home. It may have nothing whatsoever to do with the nationality, the topography, the century, or the fashion of the time. It may just be that somebody loved pink. Well, why not. You go girl! Fresco the walls, paint the ceilings, pink the fireplace, it's your home, make it your own. So my challenge, and my delight, over the coming years, will be to take this new home, and love this new home, and love its heights, and its views, and its cool marbleness, and yes, its pinkness. And make these, my own.

Appendix II

Simple Italian Cooking

I am very interested in cooking and I have a ton of cookbooks. They line half of the worktops in my kitchen. Having said that, I am very interested in cooking Italian without a cookbook. Just use a bit of nous and some imagination. In the scorching/glacial conditions of my Colli kitchen, I began to simplify my life and my cooking, because, although the dining room was vaulted and incredibly graceful, it adjoined the rather small, mean-spirited space designated as my kitchen, filled with Things Which Did Not Work. At one stage everything I prepared was fried, microwaved, or raw.

But still, we had some bang-up super meals. The fresh Italian ingredients were so great. If you found yourself drooling with anticipation in the shop, and tummy-rumbling in the car, you couldn't help but be crazed with expectation by the time you came to actually prepare it, so it would be bound to be delicious.

I have included some of my favourite Italian preparations, some gleaned from Italy, some from my previous incarnation as a caterer. You may be wondering how authentic they are. Well, what can I say? I'm a Californian from Wales cooking in Lazio. And remember: I do own all those cookbooks...

I have made them as simple as possible to tempt the timorous.

ICED COFFEE

Make a double batch of coffee at breakfast time and when it has cooled refrigerate it and when you want some put some milk in it. Simple. Starbucks is a globally successful industry but you don't have to do things their way.

TUSCAN BREAD SOUP (PAPPA AL POMODORO)

Sauté some of your favourite Mediterranean vegetables in some olive oil and then stir in some chicken stock with some passata. Toss in some torn chunks of firm stale bread like ciabatta, give it a stir and put the lid on and leave it for a bit. I like to put Parmesan in it. And maybe some torn fresh basil leaves.

TUSCAN BREAD SALAD (PANZANELLA)

The same idea but without liquid. I would serve the soup in winter and the salad in summer. Tear the stale bread into chunks and toss with your favourite sautéed Mediterranean vegetables, adding extra virgin olive oil. Grab fistfuls of very ripe tomatoes and squeeze them with your hands, letting the juice and jelly run into the bowl, and then chuck in the torn tomato skins as well. The acid in the ripe tomatoes plus the olive oil makes your dressing, and if you feel like it season with salt, pepper, torn fresh basil and Parmesan. Let it sit for a bit to let the flavours mingle. (Many people will suggest you include anchovy which gives it a real tang but I don't because I'm not really a tangy person. You can get a different sort of tang with marinated olives.) All sorts of things end up in my Panzanella which may not be authentic but are in the spirit of Italian thrift: using up leftovers in the fridge. A bit of cold chicken, perhaps, cooked pancetta, poached salmon, avocado, hard-boiled egg slices. It's very user-friendly.

CAPONATA

Confession time: I'm not a big fan of caponata but I make it from time to time because Peter loves it. When we used to live in London we could pop down the street to Carluccios and get some – theirs is brilliant – but now that we're in North Wales I make it myself.

This is the big deal with caponata: salting the aubergines. I usually make mine using recipes from old cookbooks, which tell you to salt your aubergines to remove bitterness. What a pain. But if you look online, the modern attitude is that over the years, vegetable growers have bred the bitterness out of aubergines so you only need to salt for flavour, not to remove bitterness. Also, aubergines are thirsty for oil. You can go through a ton of olive oil if you're not careful.

If you woke me up in the middle of the night and I wasn't thinking clearly I might say to you that caponata is just ratatouille with aubergine. But if you asked me again, over a big cup of coffee at breakfast, and I had my wits about me, I would tell you that it is ratatouille with aubergine and a sweet and sour sauce, which of course now doesn't make it anything like ratatouille. And ratatouille is French anyway and caponata is Sicilian. If you look at a map of Italy you will see that Sicily is right down at the bottom of The Italian Boot, in the hot, dry, arid olive-oil infused part of the country. And if you look at Sicily's neighbours you will see why suddenly you are getting sweet and sour sauces and additions like raisins. You are very, very far away from France now and the influences are different. Fruit is used with meat down here, and with vegetables. Think Moroccan tagine: that's what I'm talking about. Oh, and the pine kernels, or pine nuts as some people call them although they are seeds not nuts. If you're buying pine kernels to make pesto then buy double so you can make a proper caponata.

Now I had heard a rumour about not using pine kernels from China because they had pesticides in them which occasionally made them taste metallic. So I thought I'd fact check before telling you this, and it opened up a whole online can of worms about that metallic taste – and does it come from China or the nut itself or the person who eats it – and I've written now far more than I had ever planned about caponata. I like the advice that if you want to be pine nut avoidant just use walnuts or aim for Italian pine nuts and see for yourself.

Oh, I nearly forgot to give you the recipe....

Use your, by now very familiar, soffrito base and add your favourite Mediterranean vegetables which will of course now include a generous dollop of cubed aubergine. For the sweet and sour sauce I use honey and balsamic vinegar. Green olives look great and give texture to what could be a squidgy mass if you just use the traditional soft combination of peppers/tomatoes/zucchini/onion. Add raisins and pine kernels, and a few capers if you're really going for zing. My son has a nut allergy but apparently pine kernels are okay for him because they are a kernel/ seed not a nut, but it's never an issue because he doesn't like caponata anyway. If you suffer from nut allergies, I would be safe rather than sorry and leave the pine kernels out or take medical advice. All of the cautions and asides which I have put in about this recipe make it sound absolutely terrifying. It is, actually, a joy and delight, is caponata, when made with care, and for someone you love.

GRILLED MARINATED ROAST PEPPERS

My Italian kitchen had high ceilings but I couldn't figure out how to open the windows because they had grilles on them so imagine my delight to learn that you didn't have to grill your peppers to get that delightfully smoky, soft massed effect, you just had to peel them with a vegetable peeler before cutting them up, and then pan fry them and bingo! They were just as nice but didn't involve any violations of the Clean Air Act, and didn't make the kitchen terribly hot. A long low cook in olive oil, and then a splash of vinegar at the end: gorgeous.

CHICKEN SCALLOPINI

Please observe all safe food handling practices when preparing raw poultry and meat products

Flatten skinless, boneless chicken breasts between two sheets of greaseproof paper, banging carefully using a rolling pin. Fry them gently on both sides in olive oil (and some dried herbs if you're feeling extravagant) and give it all a good squeeze of lemon before serving. Some people like to dredge the chicken in flour first and some people like to deglaze the pan with white wine afterwards, but if you're wearing a parka and a bobble hat while cooking the meal you don't really want to hang about so nobody would condemn you if you decided to keep it simple.

STUFFED VEGETABLES:

Zucchini: Sauté some soffritto* mix and stuff it gently into zucchini which have had the insides scraped out like little boats. Top with grated Parmesan cheese and bake for a little bit, in a moderate oven.

Peppers: Halve some big peppers and take out the membrane and the seeds. Stuff with your favourite fillings, like cooked seasoned sausage meat or soffritto mix, and some breadcrumbs just for fun if you have any. Bake for a bit in a moderate oven, sprinkled with Parmesan cheese.

Tomatoes: Use some nice big plum tomatoes, cut a lid off the tomato and carefully scoop out the inside jelly and membrane. Fill with your favourite filling and bake in a moderate oven. It's tempting to reach for those ginormous beefcake tomatoes in the shops, but I find they can often be bland because they have been pumped up with water. I'd much rather have two smaller plum tomatoes which are better flavour.

Mushrooms: Portobello mushrooms are great for stuffing. Store bought mushrooms can be wiped clean with a slightly damp piece of kitchen paper. Foraged wild mushrooms need rinsing and wiping. Try not to soak them or they'll get water-logged.

Trim the cut end of the stem and dice it to add to whatever your filling is going to be. Store mushrooms in the fridge in brown paper bags to make them last longer without going slimy. Cook at a high heat, 200c, so they don't release their moisture and stew. Favourite fillings include breadcrumbs, fresh herbs, cooked seasoned sausage meat, Pecorino or Parmesan cheese, and soffritto. Mushrooms with gorgonzola and balsamic glaze make me swoon.

OH HEY LOOK! Suddenly you've got a meal! Look at that! STUFFED VEGETABLES! Stuffed zucchini, stuffed peppers, stuffed tomatoes, stuffed mushrooms.

Who would've thought?

BURRATA AND MOZZARELLA

Wherever you might want to use buffalo mozzarella, raise the game a bit by using burrata instead, (which is actually a little odd since burrata is a by-product of mozzarella production but it's so creamy it does add a really elegant flair to any dish). There was a guy used to come up from Campania every Thursday morning and sell burrata out of the boot of his car and somehow we totally trusted him because it was such an odd thing to be selling out of the boot of your car how could it possibly not be totally wonderful and authentic? We called him "Burrata Guy".

I was in a fantastic hotel in Naples once, the San Francisco al Monte. Their pool and al fresco restaurant were on the top floor, which required using the lift. I remember standing there wrapped in my towel, sharing the lift with a chap coming up from the kitchen with bags of freshly made buffalo mozzarella balls. I became conflicted, right there in the lift: to swim first, or eat buffalo mozzarella for the rest of the morning in the restaurant.

I love burrata with:

Grilled Mediterranean vegetables
Crispy bacon/pancetta and a pea & pea shoot salad
Roast butternut squash
Cherries, chocolate fondue, and roasted mixed salted nuts
As a substitute for mozzarella in traditional Caprese salad

SEAFOOD RISOTTO

Make risotto in the traditional way, and towards the end of the cooking time add cooked prawns and a good swig of passata, maybe some cayenne or some lemon if you're feeling flash.

BRUSHCETTA

I adore bruschetta, but I find that because I love the toppings so much I always over-top them and everything falls off and I get little olive oil stains down the front of my clothing which I hate.

So: make thick chunky pastes or sauces out of your ingredients and they'll stick onto the bread better. Don't over-process them as it's nice to have lots of texture. For example, roast pepper paste, mushroom paste, prawn paste, salsa instead of fresh tomatoes, black olive paste, smoked salmon paste

ANTIPASTI PLATTERS

Quintessentially Italian and quintessentially simple. I made a lot of these in my kitchen on hot days. It's impressive to have a huge display for parties and get-togethers, combining lots of different flavours and colours, but for dining à deux I prefer to have just one or two choices of really great products. This is where combining fresh and larder ingredients really comes into its own. One or two cured meats with a fresh cheese is classic, as are marinaded vegetables with fresh or aged cheese. Our local cheese was Pecorino Romano, which is saltier than its popular Parmesan cousin, so I would tend to pair it with fruit rather than cured meat. A wedge of fresh Pecorino Romano with sliced sweet peaches or grilled fresh figs drizzled with honey is magical.

Also, mixing fresh and prepared elements avoids the temptation to have too many strong flavours competing on the same plate. Too many cured meats can clash with too many marinated vegetables.

You really can't beat a simple cured meat or fish, a fresh cheese, vegetables, and a bit of crusty bread, with good quality olive oil and maybe a splash of balsamic vinegar. Plainly cooked chicken gives you scope to add fully-flavoured accompaniments.

RAIDING THE LARDER

I always had a good supply of prepared larder ingredients for days when the stresses of sorting our house difficulties made me too tired to cook....

Tinned tuna, or albacore, with tinned, drained cannellini beans and some marinated vegetables is quick and easy. Tuna and beans are mild and pick up the flavours of other elements in a dish, so this is the time to add sparkle and visual interest with marinated peppers, olives, roasted garlic, mushrooms, lemon juice or pungent herbs.

Ready-cooked lentils are also helpful for quick meals, combined with marinated artichoke hearts, olives, peppers, and sharp cheeses, or chunks of ham or sausage.

I've seen many formal recipes for risi e bisi (rice and peas), but it's actually a great opportunity to add all manner of fresh and marinated elements to add flavour and colour, with just a smidgen of oil and vinegar to tie it all together.

Pasta is, of course, the jewel in the crown of Italian cuisine, and its many shapes and names could fill a book on its own. Pairing the correct pasta shape to the correct companion sauce is key. For years I used to think that fresh pasta was superior to dried pasta in some way, because I have always valued fresh food over prepared, but honestly, fresh pasta isn't better than dried pasta, it's just different. Feel it, hold it in your hand, you can tell what sort of accompanying elements work best with it.

CANAPÉS

I actually quite like Little Things on Sticks but I hate making them. I get bored with assembly line food really quickly. Peter, bless him, used to help me out with the Little Things on Sticks when I was catering for a crowd, for which I am eternally grateful. But they do have their place in entertaining, as they are very portable when going on a picnic, or carting a meal outside onto the terrace. To a certain extent they are also more hygienic in the sense that you don't have people fingering through a bowl of food, rummaging for their next morsel. Anything you can assemble in a salad, in theory, can be stuffed on a stick. Bit of cheese, bit of meat, bit of veg, and bang! You're there. Mozzarella, tomato, basil: sorted.

BREAD

A final word about a caterer's best friend, bread. The wholemeal versions are obviously much healthier (in the shop, lift various loaves of bread and you will find that the heavier breads are the healthier breads). Gluten-free breads are a healthy option although I find that the lack of gluten makes them fall apart. But that might just be me.

The local breads in Colli were dense in texture and unsalted. They would fry up like a dream and toast beautifully. I guess I would describe them as sourdough. But the best tip I've come across for serving bread is that tearing bread, rather than slicing it, breaks open the little chambers of air pockets inside, which makes it more flavourful than slicing the bread and sealing the air pockets. I love this idea (although I can't vouch for its accuracy because the whole piece of bread goes down red lane eventually anyway), but I do prefer to take large ciabatta loaves, warm them through, and tear them into big chunks before serving in a bread basket. Don't worry about having leftovers because it's the perfect excuse to make your aforementioned TUSCAN BREAD SOUP, or its summertime equivalent, TUSCAN BREAD SALAD. Or crostini. Or bruschetta.

It's very Italian to be economical with your shopping; waste not want not.

FLAVOURED OILS AND VINEGAR

I always have garlic-infused olive oil on hand, which may be Lazy Italian but I don't really like fiddling with garlic cloves and garlic peelers very much and then having garlicky finger tips afterwards. Basil-infused oil is lovely if you struggle to keep a fresh pot of basil happy on your kitchen windowsill. Lemon oil is gorgeous on fish and in salads, which I could use more often if I didn't like using fresh lemon so much.

Chilli oil is readily available and can give you the same hit as a dash of cayenne, but I'm a Bland Food Person when it comes to heat so I rarely use it, but again, that's just me. Feel free. Go for the heat.

Whenever I need vinegar I usually reach for balsamic unless the colour dictates that I need white. Occasionally I can pick up white balsamic vinegar in shops, but I really wouldn't want to get into a hefty dinner table debate about white balsamic vs. traditional white wine vinegar because I'm just not that up on the subject. To my mind, very little in life cannot be improved with a streak of balsamic glaze over it.

*SOFFRITTO

A diced vegetable base made up of carrot, onion and celery. You can buy ready- made frozen soffritto from some high street supermarkets. It might be called classic vegetable base mix. It will usually be a very fine dice which is great as a basis for soups and stews. If you want your Italian recipes to have a bit of chunky texture then I would make your own soffritto base so that the ingredients in the soffritto are the same size as other ingredients in your dish, which I think is very nice but might not matter that much to other people.

Special Thanks

I would like to give special thanks to my very supportive family,
who have stood by me as I have written this trio of memoirs.
Thanks to my lovely sons, who have graciously allowed me to
write publicly about their adventures, and their follies.
Thanks to my loving and long-suffering husband Peter
for his help and understanding.
Thanks to Cecilia Gatehouse for her ethereal artwork,
which has graced all three book covers in this series.
Thanks to my long-time friend Susan Peatfield, whose
encouragement for my writing got the whole thing rolling.
And to my editor and friend Jac Tobin, who has actually
gotten everything done-and-dusted, and down on the page.
I feel truly blessed to be backed by this small, but mighty, team.

MARCIE LAYTON

Marcie Layton is a memoirist, living in North Wales. She writes about Wales, her family, travel in Italy, and her experience of life on the autistic spectrum. Previously published work includes 'Fi 'di'r Deinosor', in the short story anthology *Zero Hours on the Boulevard*, published by Parthian books, her 2021 memoir *A Life Lived Behind Glass: A Journey through the Autistic Spectrum* and her follow-up memoir *Cwtch* about *A Life Loved in Wales*. The memoir you're reading now completes the trilogy.

Photo: Andrew Nash

Printed in Great Britain
by Amazon

67206635R00129